Toward More Efficient and Effective Public Social Spending in Central America

DIRECTIONS IN DEVELOPMENT
Human Development

Toward More Efficient and Effective Public Social Spending in Central America

Pablo A. Acosta, Rita Almeida, Thomas Gindling, and Christine Lao Peña

WORLD BANK GROUP

Contents

Table

Foreword

This book touches on an important and timely topic for Central American countries: how to improve public budget allocation to, and spending in, social sectors, which are essential to promoting a better standard of living for current and future citizens, especially those who are poor and vulnerable.

In order to assess the effectiveness and efficiency of social public spending, this book carries out a detailed analysis of public spending trends and composition in the social sectors (education, health, and social protection and labor) between 2007 and 2014. It also reviews the quality of selected institutions and sector governance arrangements that influence public social spending. The book addresses three crucial policy issues: (a) how to improve the coverage and redistributional incidence of public social spending, (b) how to enhance the effectiveness and efficiency of public social spending, and (c) how to strengthen the institutions governing public spending in the social sector.

This book builds on already published, country-specific social sector expenditure and institutional reviews in six countries (Costa Rica, El Salvador, Guatemala, Honduras, Nicaragua, and Panama), produced by the same World Bank Group team over the past three years. In addition, using recent empirical studies and analyses, it provides comparisons with other countries in Latin America and with other regions, which complement its subregional review.

The conclusions are rich in concrete policy recommendations for education, health, and social protection and labor across the different countries. Several recommendations are country specific because they depend on each country's context. However, all six countries share three main areas for improvement. First, there is an urgent need to strengthen the monitoring and evaluation system of the three social sectors to promote more cost-effective spending. Only with more and better data to track performance in terms of social outputs and outcomes, as well as resource flows and costs, at the country and subnational levels can the subregion monitor and evaluate programs and the effectiveness of public social spending. Second, it is equally important to foster increased accountability of public service providers at the national and subnational levels for achieving human development outputs and outcomes. Finally, improved coordination in the design, implementation, and delivery of social interventions is critical to achieving more effective results, as well as to supporting the availability of more-qualified human resources.

This book is highly recommended reading for policy makers who are implementing public policies in social sectors, as well as for members of the general public who are interested in learning about the progress made by governments and the challenges that they face in responding to the pressing demand for better social sector delivery in Central America.

J. Humberto Lopez
Country Director, Central America
World Bank

Acknowledgments

A team led by Pablo Acosta, Rita Almeida, Tim Gindling, and Christine Lao Peña prepared this book. The authors give special thanks to Emma Monsalve Montiel and Valeria Vargas Sejas for outstanding assistance in several stages, including analytical and empirical analysis; to Angela Maria Rubio for support in formatting; and to Diane Stamm for editing services.

The authors thank Tania Dmytraczenko, Daniel Dulitzky, Margaret Grosh, and Reema Nayar for comments and overall guidance; Lars Sondergaard for helpful suggestions; and all task team leaders and team members in the Central America Human Development cluster who, in different ways, contributed with useful discussions and inputs to earlier versions and in preparing the individual country notes.

About the Authors

Pablo A. Acosta is a senior economist in the Social Protection and Labor Global Practice of the World Bank. An Argentinean national, he holds a Ph.D. in economics from the University of Illinois at Urbana-Champaign in the United States. He joined the World Bank as a young professional in 2008 and, since then, has worked in three regions: Africa (2009–10), Latin America and the Caribbean (2010–15), and East Asia and Pacific (since 2015). Prior to joining the World Bank, he worked at Corporacion Andina de Fomento (Latin American Development Bank), the Inter-American Development Bank, the Ministry of Economy in Argentina, and the Foundation for Latin American Economic Research.

Acosta's main areas of expertise are conditional cash transfers, public works, labor policies, migration, and skills development. He has written several peer-reviewed articles, which have been published in journals that include the following: *Journal of International Economics, Labour Economics, Economic Development and Cultural Change, World Development, Journal of Development Studies,* and *World Economy*, among others. He has also contributed chapters to several World Bank publications. More recently, in 2016, he coauthored the World Bank book titled *Minds and Behaviors at Work: Boosting Socioemotional Skills for Latin America's Workforce*. He is also a research fellow at the Institute for the Study of Labor, and an associate editor for *EconomiA*, a Brazilian economic journal.

Rita Almeida is a senior economist in the World Bank's Education Global Practice. Since joining the World Bank in 2002, Almeida has led policy dialogue on a diverse set of regions and countries, including Latin America, Eastern Europe, and the Middle East and North Africa. Prior to joining the World Bank, Almeida worked in a private investment bank and lectured at the Portuguese Catholic University. Her main areas of expertise cover labor market analysis, skills development policies, activation and graduation policies, labor market regulations, social protection for workers, firm productivity and innovation policies, public expenditure reviews and the evaluation of social programs. Over the years, Almeida has led and contributed to several World Bank flagship publications. More recently, she coauthored the book, *The Right Skills for the Job? Rethinking*

Training Policies for Workers, which examines the conditions for effective design and implementation of skills development policies in different country contexts. Her academic work has been published in a variety of top general-interest and specialized journals, including *The Economic Journal, American Economic Journal: Applied Economics, Journal of International Economics, Labour Economics,* and *World Development.* A Portuguese national, Almeida holds a Ph.D. in economics from Universitat Pompeu Fabra, Spain. She has been a fellow of the Institute for the Study of Labor since 2003.

Tim Gindling is a professor of economics and public policy at the University of Maryland Baltimore County and has been a Fulbright Scholar and visiting faculty member at the University of Costa Rica and the National Autonomous University of Costa Rica. He has also served as a consultant to Central American governments and international development institutions such as the World Bank. His primary research interests are studies of labor markets, social policy, poverty, and income inequality in Central America. Gindling's research has been published in peer-reviewed journals such as *World Development, Economic Development and Cultural Change, Journal of Development Studies, Economics of Education Review, Latin American Research Review, CEPAL Review, Mesoamerican, IIZA Journal of Labor Studies, Industrial and Labor Relations Review,* and *Labour Economics.* Recent peer-reviewed publications include "The Distribution of Income in Central America"; "South-South Migration: The Impact of Nicaraguan Immigrants on Earnings, Inequality and Poverty in Costa Rica"; "Self-Employment in the Developing World"; "The Consequences of Increased Enforcement of Legal Minimum Wages in Costa Rica"; and six other articles on the impact of legal minimum wages on employment, earnings, poverty, and income inequality in Costa Rica, El Salvador, Honduras and Nicaragua. Gindling holds a Ph.D. in economics from Cornell University in Ithaca, New York. He has been a research fellow of the Institute for the Study of Labor since 2007.

Christine Lao Peña is a senior human development economist in the World Bank's Health, Nutrition, and Population Global Practice. She has extensive operational experience in social sector projects in several countries in Africa and in Latin America and the Caribbean. Her current work focuses on health financing and innovations in health service delivery including results-based management mechanisms and multisectoral approaches to improving maternal and child nutrition and health, mainly in the Latin America and Caribbean region. Before joining the World Bank, Lao Peña was at the International Food Policy Research Institute, where she worked on intrahousehold and nutrition and food security issues. She also worked at the University of the Philippines on a number of applied research topics including nontariff barriers to trade in local food and transportation. She has more than 20 years of applied research experience on a broad range of topics, with an emphasis on health, nutrition, early childhood development, gender, and poverty. She has published book chapters, papers, and journal articles on health program reviews; intrahousehold resource allocation; and gender, food security, and development. A Filipino national, she has a Ph.D. and M.A. in economics from Boston University.

Abbreviations

ALMP	active labor market program
CA	Central America
CBI	cognitive-behavioral intervention
CCSS	Caja Costarricense de Seguridad Social (Costa Rican Social Security Institute)
CCT	conditional cash transfer
CENISS	Centro Nacional de Información del Sector Social (National Center for Information on the Social Sector)
CEPAL	Comisión Económica para América Latina (Economic Commission for Latin America and the Caribbean)
CNU	Consejo Nacional Universitario (National University Council)
COSAM	Comando de Sanidad Militar (Military Health Unit)
CSS	Caja de Seguro Social (Social Security Council)
DHS	Demographic Health Survey
EBAIS	Equipo Básico de Atención Integral de Salud (Basic Team for Integrated Health Care)
ECAP	Evaluación de las Competencias Acádemicas y Pedagógicas (Evaluation of Academic Competencies and Pedagogy
ECH	Encuesta Continua de Hogares (Continuous Household Survey)
ECOS	Equipo Comunitario de Salud (Family Community Team)
EdStats	Education Statistics Database (of the World Bank)
EDUCO	Educación con Participación de la Comunidad (Education with Community Participation)
EEC	Estrategia de Extensión de Cobertura (Strategy for Coverage Extension)
EHPM	Encuesta de Hogares de Propósitos Múltiples (Multiple Purpose Household Survey)
EML	Encuesta del Mercado Laboral (Labor Market Survey)
EMNV	Encuesta de Medicion de Niveles de Vida (Welfare Measurement Survey)

ENAHO	Encuesta Nacional de Hogares (National Household Survey)
ENCOVI	Encuesta Nacional de Condiciones de Vida (National Survey of Life Conditions)
ENSA	Encuesta Nacional de Salud (National Health Survey)
ENV	Encuesta Nacional de Niveles de Vida
ERCA	Programa Estado de la Región (State of Central American Region)
FTS	full-time school
GDP	gross domestic product
ICEFI	Instituto Centroamericano de Estudios Fiscales (Central American Institute for Fiscal Studies)
IGSS	Instituto Guatemalteco de Seguridad Social (Guatemalan Institute of Social Security)
IMAS	Instituto Mixta de Ayuda Social (Mixed Institute of Social Aid)
IMF	International Monetary Fund
INA	Instituto Nacional de Aprendizaje (National Apprentice Institute)
INATEC	Instituto Nacional Tecnológico (National Institute of Technology)
INFOP	Instituto Nacional de Formación Profesional (National Institute for Professional Training)
INSAFORP	Instituto Salvadoreño de Formación Profesional (Salvadoran Institute for Professional Training)
INTECAP	Instituto Técnico de Capacitación y Productividad (Technical Training and Productivity Institute)
LAC	Latin America and the Caribbean
LLECE	Latin American Laboratory for Assessment of the Quality of Education
MIDES	Ministry of Social Development
MIFAPRO	Mi Familia Progresa (My Family Progresses)
MINED	Ministry of Education
MMR	maternal mortality ratio
MOH	Ministry of Health
NCD	noncommunicable disease
NEET	neither in school nor employed nor in training
NGO	nongovernmental organization
ODEI	Organismo Directivo de la Escuela Inclusiva
OECD	Organisation for Economic Co-operation and Development
PADEP/D	Professional In-service Teacher Training Program

PAESITA	Prueba de Aprendizajes y Aptitudes para Egresados de Educación Básica (National Assessment of Learning Competencies for Basic Education Graduates)
PAISS	Paquete Integral de Servicios de Salud (Integrated Package of Health Care Services)
PATI	Programa de Apoyo Temporal al Ingreso (Temporary Income Support Program)
PEN	Programa Estado de la Nación (State of the Nation Program)
PHC	primary health care
PIRLS	Progress in International Reading Literacy Study
PISA	Programme for International Student Assessment
PPP	purchasing power parity
PRONADE	Programa Nacional de Autogestión para el Desarrollo Educativo
PSE	public sector efficiency
PSP	public sector performance
PSPV	Programa de Proteccion de Salud para Poblacion Vulnerable (Health Protection for Vulnerable Populations Program)
RBF	results-based financing
RIIS	Red Integral e Integrada de Servicios de Salud (Network of Integrated Health Care Services)
ROI	Registro de Oferta Institucional
RUB	Registro Único de Beneficiarios (Unique Beneficiary Registry)
SABE	Sistema de Atención a Beneficiarios (Beneficiary Attention System)
SBM	school-based management
SDS	Secretaría de Desarrollo Social (Secretary of Social Development)
SEDUC	Secretaría de Estado en el Despacho de Educación (Ministry of Education)
SERCE	Second Regional Comparative and Explanatory Study
SPL	social protection and labor
SSEIR	social sector expenditure and institutional review
SUEPPS	Sistema Único de Evaluación de Políticas Públicas Sociales (Unified System for the Evaluation of Social Public Policies)
TERCE	Third Regional Comparative and Explanatory Study
TIMSS	Trends in Mathematics and Science Study
UNESCO	United Nations Educational, Scientific, and Cultural Organization

Executive Summary

Overview

This report looks at the trends in public social spending in Central America from 2007 to 2014, conducts international benchmarking, examines measures of the effectiveness and efficiency of social spending, and assesses the quality of selected institutions influencing public social spending. We consider social spending to be public spending that is allocated to the education, health, and social protection and labor (SPL) sectors. The report recognizes that Central American countries receive funding for and support to social sectors from donors, nongovernmental organizations (NGOs), and private institutions that influences social services provision in the sector, but this report focuses on public social spending. In analyzing public social spending, the report addresses three crucial policy issues: (a) how to improve the coverage and redistributional incidence of public social spending, (b) how to enhance the effectiveness and efficiency of public social spending, and (c) how to strengthen the institutions governing public spending in the social sector.

While based heavily on a series of recent analytical social spending studies in six countries in the subregion—Costa Rica, El Salvador, Guatemala, Honduras, Nicaragua, and Panama—this report also takes a broader regional perspective and includes some comparisons to countries in other regions. The overview report builds on a series of country-level documents, the Social Sector Expenditure and Institutional Reviews (SSEIR), from these six countries in the subregion. In addition, we incorporate recent empirical studies of the efficiency and effectiveness of education, health, and SPL spending in Latin America and around the world to inform our discussions of the issues and policy recommendations.

We make several important contributions. First, we contribute to an extensive set of regional analytical work and cross-sector work conducted recently by the World Bank by providing new evidence regarding the coverage, distribution, effectiveness, and efficiency of social public spending in the subregion. A significant value-added of this report is to compare the trends, levels, and within-country distribution of social spending in relation to coverage, distribution, and effectiveness of social services (for example, enrollments in school, access to health care, and targeting of cash transfers) to identify where public social spending is most efficient. Second, we provide benchmarks for indicators of social sector performance by comparing Central American countries with Latin America as a whole and with other countries at similar levels of income per capita. Third, we identify institutional and governing structures that promote or impede the efficiency and effectiveness of public social services. This is done by describing the institutional and governing structure of public spending in the social sector and then comparing this to the coverage and effectiveness of social spending.

For this report, new spending data were collected, harmonized, and analyzed, focusing not only on overall social spending but also going into more detail on the education, health, and SPL sectors. The aggregate social spending data used correspond to the budget executed by centralized and decentralized government entities and follow the International Monetary Fund (IMF) classification. Spending data were harmonized to capture the same items in a consistent and systematic manner across countries. For example, education spending includes public spending on primary, secondary (lower and upper), and tertiary education plus other educational institutions delivering public education services in the countries. Health spending includes medical services (outpatient and inpatient in hospitals and clinics), public health services, health research, and other health spending. SPL spending includes social security pensions, disability, cash transfers, general subsidies and other social assistance, and active labor market programs (ALMPs) and policies.

The report relies on multiple data sources. Social sector expenditure data come primarily from the Instituto Centroamericano de Estudios Fiscales (Central American Institute for Fiscal Studies, ICEFI), which was tasked with collecting official fiscal national and subnational spending data for each country for 2007–14 and harmonizing them following the IMF classification for comparability. Information on institutional and governance structure was collected during country missions and through reports written by local consultants familiar with each country's institutional environment. Evidence on coverage, distribution, and effectiveness of social spending comes primarily from several household surveys and sector-specific data collected by the social line ministries and partners across the six countries, covering 2005–14.

Main Findings

Central American countries are all relatively small in population, area, and size of economies; have a common history and culture; and share many of the same human development problems. Some examples of shared problems include high secondary school dropout rates, challenges in providing health coverage to the entire population, large informal sectors, and inflexible and inefficient institutions and governance in the social sectors. In other ways, the countries are very different. For example, El Salvador, Guatemala, Nicaragua, and Honduras have all had recent and violent civil conflicts; this contrasts with Panama and Costa Rica, which do not even have national armies.

Even though the civil wars ended in the 1990s, the aftermaths continue to exert a negative impact on human development. Youth and gang violence continue to be a serious public safety and human development issue in El Salvador, Guatemala, and Honduras, but not in Costa Rica, Nicaragua, or Panama. In Costa Rica, El Salvador, and Panama, lower secondary completion rates are high while dropouts in upper secondary are a problem. In Guatemala, Honduras, and Nicaragua, dropout rates are high in both lower and upper secondary.

Health indicators differ significantly among countries. Costa Rica's indicators are similar to those of countries belonging to the Organization for Economic Co-operation and Development (OECD) and are among the highest in Latin America and the Caribbean (LAC), while Guatemala's health indicators, especially among the indigenous population, are among the lowest in LAC.

In economic terms, most Central American countries are middle income, but Nicaragua has the second-lowest gross domestic product (GDP) per capita in LAC (after Haiti). With the exception of Panama, economic growth in Central America has been slow. From 2007 to 2014, real average annual per capita GDP growth in Panama was 6 percent, compared to 2 percent in Costa Rica and Nicaragua, 1 percent in Guatemala and Honduras, and 0.75 percent in El Salvador. Over the same period, the average annual per capita GDP growth rate in LAC overall was approximately 1.5 percent. Poverty rates in 2014 range from 12 percent in Costa Rica to 41.4 percent in Nicaragua, 55.9 percent in Honduras, and 59.8 percent in Guatemala.

Public spending in the social sectors can contribute to reducing poverty and inequality, but the impact of social spending in Central America is less than it could be not just because of the overall low level of allocated resources but because of the inefficiencies identified in this report. Between 2007 and 2014, poverty rates fell more slowly in Central America than in LAC as a whole. Progress in reducing poverty in Central America was slow in part because most Central American countries grew more slowly than the LAC average, but also because the economic growth that did occur had a smaller impact on poverty in Central America than in the rest of LAC.

One reason for the limited impact of economic growth on poverty is inefficiencies in the provision of public social services. Another is low overall levels of public social spending. Public spending has grown in recent years; as a percentage of GDP, between 2007 and 2014, public social spending increased in Costa Rica, El Salvador, Guatemala, and Nicaragua, but fell in Honduras and Panama. Levels of social spending are still low, however, and limit the ability of social programs to have large impacts. Except for Costa Rica, total per capita social spending levels in Central America are still low compared to other countries in LAC. Expressed in 2005 dollars, in 2012 per capita social spending was US$1,325 in Costa Rica, US$489 in Panama, US$443 in El Salvador, US$184 in Honduras, US$179 in Guatemala, and US$157 in

Nicaragua, compared to US$1,413 in Chile, US$1,402 in Brazil, US$905 in Mexico, and US$489 in Colombia.

The focus of social spending also varied among Central American countries. Social security pension spending is the largest part of social spending in Costa Rica, where it reached 14 percent of total public spending in 2014, and in Honduras, where it reached 13 percent of total public spending that year. Health and education spending is a big part of social spending in each country. Public spending on health ranged from 2.2 percent of GDP in Guatemala to 5.6 percent in Costa Rica in 2014. Education spending is highest in Costa Rica (5.5 percent of GDP in 2014) and Honduras (5.4 percent in 2014), and falls to 4 percent in Nicaragua, 3.6 percent in El Salvador, 3.4 percent in Panama, and 2.9 percent in Guatemala. SPL is the smallest part of social spending (less than 2.6 percent of GDP in all countries), but is increasing as a percentage of GDP in all countries except Panama.

Between 2007 and 2014, total social spending as a percentage of GDP and as a percentage of total public spending, increased in Costa Rica, Guatemala and Nicaragua, while social security spending as a percentage of total public spending fell in all other Central American countries. As a percentage of GDP, education spending increased in all Central American countries between 2007 and 2014, with the largest increase in Costa Rica (from 3.9 percent of GDP in 2007 to 5.5 percent in 2014). Between 2007 and 2014, the share of public spending on health as a percentage of total public spending increased in all Central American countries except El Salvador and Honduras.

In education, Central American countries have made considerable progress, with near-universal primary coverage rates and important gains in preprimary and secondary enrollments, but gaps in access remain especially in preprimary and completion of secondary levels, and learning outcomes across the whole education system tend to be very low. The sub-region has also been characterized by some heterogeneity in consolidating the progress for primary as shown by the fall in enrollments for primary education in Guatemala. Secondary completion rates for those aged 25 and older are 35.4 percent in LAC as a whole but only 27.7 percent in Central America. Furthermore, inefficiencies in public spending have limited gains in key indicators. For example, repetition rates and overage indicators are high relative to comparator countries. Throughout the subregion, there are poor results and low participation in international examinations assessing reading, mathematics and science, suggesting that the quality of education is also weak in the region.

In health, there has been important progress, but several challenges remain. With regard to results, for example, infant mortality rates have fallen from 2007 to 2014 by 6.0 percentage points in El Salvador, 8.4 in Guatemala, 5.2 in Honduras, 5.0 in Nicaragua, and 4.3 in Panama, compared to 3.5 percentage points in LAC as a whole. In contrast, maternal mortality ratios in 2014 were higher in Guatemala (93 per 10,000 live births), Honduras (132), Nicaragua (154), and Panama (97) than in LAC as a whole (69 per 10,000 live births). Noncommunicable diseases have also emerged as being among the leading causes of deaths in these countries.

For most countries in the sub-region, however, curative care particularly spending in hospitals account for a significant share of public spending compared to more cost-effective preventive care and health promotion. In addition, while there have been some initiatives to improve the results orientation of public spending on health, inefficiencies exist especially in the management of human resources, medicines, and supplies. Fragmentation and insufficient coordination among health institutions also contribute to duplication of efforts and resources.

There have been enormous advances in setting up, expanding access to, and increasing spending on *social protection policies and programs* in Central America, following the broad Latin American regional trend. While the majority of public social spending in SPL in the subregion is still focused on contributory pensions, social assistance has expanded immensely, increasing in all countries in the subregion since 2007. Major innovations—the most important of which is use of poverty-targeting instruments—led to the expansion in social assistance.

Two important types of programs that have taken the space left by general subsidies are (a) social (or noncontributory) pensions, and (b) conditional cash transfers (CCTs). This report's assessment is that CCTs, in particular, are well targeted and already proving their value in terms of improving access to health and education. However, despite being in the social assistance toolkit in all countries except Nicaragua, CCT performance varies considerably, particularly in terms of the regularity and predictability of payments (a particular concern in Guatemala and Honduras) and in identifying the appropriate beneficiaries (errors of exclusion can be substantial given the small size of these programs in countries such as El Salvador). In most of Central America, ALMPs are a much smaller part of SPL spending compared to pensions and subsidies. Costa Rica is an exception (where spending on ALMPs as a percentage of GDP is similar to the OECD country average) as well as Nicaragua (for payroll-financed public training provision).

The analysis presented also suggests that there is room for improved efficiency in public social spending institutions throughout Central America. According to our estimates of efficiency and cost-effectiveness, only in Panama is overall public spending in the social sectors both efficient and moderately effective.[1] In addition, in 2013, the percentage of the allocated budget actually spent in the social sectors was only 90 percent in Costa Rica, 88 percent in Panama, 89 percent in Guatemala, and 85 percent in Honduras, suggesting possible implementation bottlenecks. Estimates of the efficiency and effectiveness of public social sectors calculated in this report also suggest that, in general, social spending in the subregion is not cost-effective.

Main Recommendations

The report discusses several ways in which public social spending can be improved in the subregion to get better results. In all sectors and Central American countries, it is important to, first, strengthen monitoring and evaluation by building in monitoring and evaluation mechanisms early on at the program design stage to track performance and have timely, reliable data for planning and decision making. Second, enhance accountability for results, including systematic enforcement of incentives and accountability measures, and ensure periodic reporting of results to citizens. Third, reallocate resources to better serve those in geographic areas with less access. Location is important; for example, access to education, health, and social protection services is lowest in rural and indigenous areas in all countries. Efforts should be strengthened to improve access in these areas. Finally, institutional arrangements are still far from being efficient, with overly complex and overlapping mandates (such as in Costa Rica) and policy reversals or lack of continuity in program implementation (e.g., in El Salvador, Guatemala). Despite general advances in improving key human development indicators, the pending agenda still looms large.

In education, first, there is room for increasing the efficiency of education spending by rebalancing public expenditure from less cost-effective to more cost-effective programs. Less cost-effective programs are traditionally more focused on school inputs (for example, textbooks or uniforms) which are often not very effective at improving learning outcomes. In addition, developing a more comprehensive and diverse strategy to reduce (secondary) school dropout rates, and improving student educational trajectories, going beyond supply-side interventions and also focusing on demand-side policies that increase the demand for schooling can be promising in the subregion. The analysis shows that the focus should be more on sustaining the gains achieved in primary and completing lower secondary for Guatemala, Honduras, and Nicaragua, and in completing upper secondary for Costa Rica, El Salvador, and Panama.

Second, there is also room to improve the efficiency of spending on basic education, as the subregion needs to improve access to high-quality early childhood education, which sets the foundation for cognitive and socioemotional skills. Today, extensive research on emerging economies shows that increased access to high-quality early childhood education will improve school readiness and retention in higher grades. In addition, efficiency of spending can improve with the support to interventions that focus on improved pedagogies, improved teacher quality, and teachers' and directors' accountability. Some promising policies to achieve this goal are "in-service" teacher training programs that address knowledge gaps and also classroom management techniques, promote quality standards through entry and exit exams for teachers, and develop and implement incentives to groom and motivate teachers (for example, effective trainings linked to career progression).

In the Central American region, spending on, and access to, tertiary education throughout the subregion is biased toward students from high-income families. For example, in Panama 42 percent of students enrolled in tertiary education are in the top income quintile, 25 percent are in the fourth quintile, and only 5 percent are in the bottom quintile. This is the opposite of the distribution of primary education, where 66 percent of students are in the bottom two quintiles. The regressiveness of this spending needs to be tackled by focusing more on quality interventions that increase quality and learning at the end of high school for all students and more demand-side programs that expand interest in, and access to, tertiary education to lower-income students. In addition, stronger subregional coordination in accreditation of tertiary education could ensure higher returns to tertiary education even if students migrate to other countries.

In health, most Central American countries have successfully expanded access to services. While access to health services fell in Guatemala since early 2015, with almost 40 percent of the population not having access to primary health care services, other Central American countries have improved coverage of essential health services. Nonetheless, regular access to health services in rural areas needs to be improved in Honduras, El Salvador, Nicaragua, and Panama. In terms of services provided, more resources would also need to be allocated to prevention and health promotion measures which are much more cost effective relative to curative care.

While coverage gaps exist for most countries, the main challenge that all Central American countries face is the need to improve the quality of care. Given that human resources is the most important health input, countries might need to reallocate more funds to provide incentives to attract and retain skilled personnel, especially in rural areas. They would also need to address staffing shortages with the strategic use of technology (for example, telemedicine). In addition, countries that have less than the required health staff (El Salvador, Guatemala, Honduras, and Nicaragua) relative to World Health Organization standards would need to coordinate with the education sector to train more health workers.

Availability of essential medicines is also an important indicator of quality of services. The reported shortages of medicines and supplies in several countries, especially in Guatemala and Honduras, also underscore the importance of improving the procurement and overall management of medicines and supplies. Countries could also use performance-based financing and strengthen monitoring and accountability mechanisms, including civil society participation in monitoring services to encourage health institutions and facilities to improve their services.

Finally, to attain universal health coverage (access to quality services based on established standards and adequate financial protection), most Central American countries would need to progressively address institutional fragmentation as reflected by insufficient coordination and differences in health benefits packages provided by public institutions, especially by their respective Ministries of Health and Social Security Institutes.

Central American social security systems, which account for the bulk of **SPL spending**, are clearly not delivering what they promised; coverage is still low and their fiscal sustainability is questionable. As in many other Latin American counties, but more so in Central America due to the higher incidence of labor informality, coverage of the contributory pension system is particularly low and regressive. At the same time, the fiscal costs of social security systems for resource-constrained governments in the Central American subregion are enormous. In some cases, this is due to generous subsidies, in particular for public sector employees who can retire with higher-than-average replacement rates.

For example, replacement rates for many public sector employees in Costa Rica and Guatemala are higher than the LAC, and even OECD country averages. In others, failed reforms did not deliver what they promised and have even generated onerous transition costs that current generations are still paying (for example, in El Salvador). Almost all pension systems in the Central American region have severe funding deficits and contingent liabilities that require urgent reforms to avoid a major drag on fiscal accounts that would crowd out other needed spending in basic delivery of social sector services or subsidies to the poor. This problem, unless tackled urgently, can become unmanageable with the aging of the population and the increase in dependency ratios (dependents over active population).

Despite advances in setting up social registries and sophisticated and objective targeting instruments, social assistance spending still needs to minimize errors of inclusion and exclusion. And despite recent reductions, universal and regressive general subsidies still weigh heavily on the fiscally challenged countries in Central America. Reforming consumption subsidies can free up resources for better-targeted and more efficient programs. However, poverty-targeted CCTs are still a small part of public social spending in most Central American countries, reaching only a small proportion of poor families. In addition, their performance has been uneven, with larger impacts in countries like El Salvador, Honduras, and Panama than in Costa Rica and Guatemala.

There are also important links between the success of CCTs and reforms in other sectors. For example, for CCTs to improve education and health outcomes, quality education and health care must be available. The lack of sustainability and fairness of contributory pension systems, which are overly generous for public sector employees and fiscally unaffordable despite lower overall coverage than in the rest of Latin America, also calls for urgent reform. Noncontributory (social) pensions are better targeted, but in all countries still cover a small proportion of the poorest (ranging from approximately 1 percent in Guatemala and Honduras, for the lowest quintile, to a high of 38 percent in Costa Rica and Nicaragua).

Finally, throughout the subregion, ALMPs cover a small fraction of target groups (that is, the young unemployed) and have not been successful in improving employment opportunities or wages for priority groups. For example, in Costa Rica there is evidence that returns to the largest ALMP, Instituto Nacional de Aprendizaje (National Apprentice Institute, INA), are much lower than private training institutions and may actually be negative. ALMPs need to be revamped and made more relevant for the unemployed population and labor market entrants.

There are several cross-sectoral recommendations to consider. The subregion needs to strengthen monitoring and evaluation systems across the social sectors. It is also critical to strengthen accountability of the public service provision to focus on "human development" results. This includes systematic enforcement of incentives and accountability measures and ensuring periodic reporting of results to citizens. It is important to know which programs are effective and efficient to direct spending to those programs and eliminate programs that are not effective.

Access to education, health, and social protection services is lower in rural and indigenous areas in all countries. Resources should be reallocated to better serve those in geographic areas with less access.

Finally, it is critical to strengthen coordination within the social sectors to increase the availability of qualified human resources. To increase the availability of qualified health sector staff, for example, the education and health sectors would need to coordinate better to enhance the practical relevance of the curriculum and teaching quality; attract more students and trainees, especially from rural, indigenous communities; and reduce dropouts.

Note

1. Efficiency is defined as public sector performance divided by public sector expenditure (see box 5.6).

CHAPTER 1

Introduction

This report documents patterns of public social spending (on education, health, and social protection and labor [SPL]) in Central America and identifies ways to improve its performance and efficiency. With the exception of Costa Rica, public social spending in the region is below the Latin American average and below other countries at similar income levels (see chapter 3 and figure 3.2). Low levels of public social spending are often accompanied by low levels of government revenues. The ratios of revenue to gross domestic product (GDP) for Costa Rica, El Salvador, Guatemala, and Honduras are below or at the average for other countries in the world with similar GDP per capita (figure 1.1). Low government revenues are due to a low tax base and high rates of tax evasion. Further, within Central America, the trend in revenues has not been upward. Between 2007 and 2014, government revenue as a percentage of GDP fell in four of the six Central American countries studies in this report, increasing only in El Salvador and Nicaragua (figure 1.2). Given tight fiscal constraints and political considerations,[1] it is unlikely that total social spending in the region can increase substantially in the near future.

In general, budget deficits have been addressed through reductions in spending and not increases in revenues (figure 1.2). Despite low levels of public social spending in many Central American countries, there is room to improve the efficiency and performance of social spending in all countries. Recognizing revenue constraints, this report focuses on the short-term goal of getting better human development results with current spending levels rather than the long-term goal of increasing total government spending and revenues.

This report addresses three key challenges facing Central America: (a) improving the coverage and redistributional incidence of public spending, (b) enhancing the effectiveness and efficiency (quality) of public social spending, and (c) strengthening the institutions governing public spending in the social sector. Social spending in the subregion is often not well targeted and is unequally distributed. We document how much is spent, whether public spending is going to the intended groups (that is, children, the poorest families, low skilled), and how

Figure 1.1 Government Revenue Compared with GDP per Capita, 2014

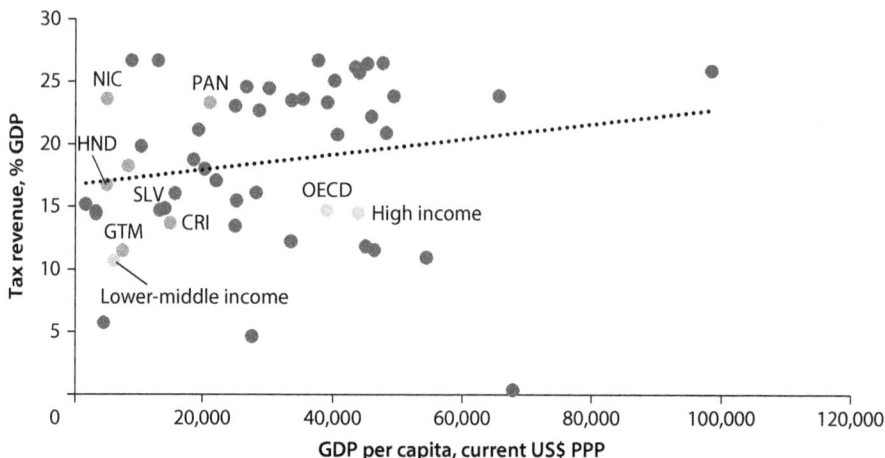

Source: World Bank, World Development Indicators database.
Note: CRI = Costa Rica; GTM = Guatemala; HND = Honduras; NIC = Nicaragua; OECD = Organisation for Economic
Co-operation and Development; PAN = Panama; SLV = El Salvador.

Figure 1.2 Changes in Revenue and Fiscal Balance (Deficit or Surplus), 2007–14

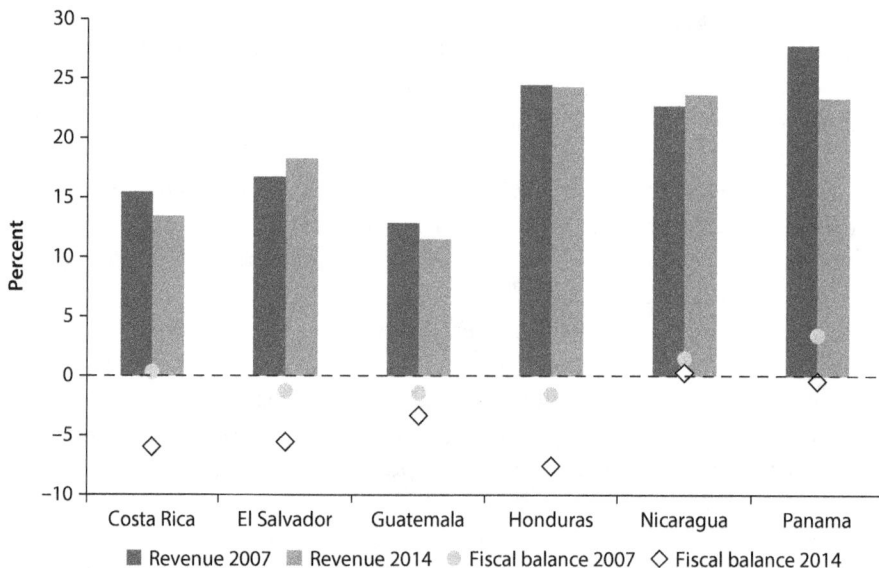

Source: International Monetary Fund, Article IV Consultations.

targeting can be improved. We identify where public social spending is, and is
not, leading to improved measurable indicators of well-being and, where appropriate, suggest ways to improve the quality of public social services. The institutions that provide and finance social services in Central America are often costly
and fragmented, with overlapping mandates, and with limited monitoring and

evaluation of the efficiency and effectiveness of social spending. Finally, we suggest potentially more efficient and cost-effective ways of delivering social services in Central America.

Although focused on analyzing public social spending in the region, the report also goes deeper into analyzing the patterns and trends in public spending in the education, health, and SPL sectors. Aggregate social spending corresponds to the budget executed by centralized and decentralized government entities and follows the IMF classification. The data were harmonized to capture the same items in a consistent and systematic manner across countries. For example, in education, spending includes public spending on primary, secondary (lower and upper), and tertiary education plus other educational institutions delivering public education services in the countries. For health, spending includes medical services (outpatient and inpatient in hospitals and clinics), public health services, health research, and other health spending. SPL spending includes social security pensions, disability, cash transfers, general subsidies and other social assistance, plus ALMPs.

This work relies on multiple administrative and survey data sources for the subregion during 2007–14. This was a challenging task given the difficulties in accessing data in the subregion. Social sector expenditure data come primarily from the Instituto Centroamericano de Estudios Fiscales (Central American Institute of Fiscal Studies, ICEFI), which collected official fiscal national and subnational spending data for each country for 2007–14 and harmonized it following the IMF classification for comparability. Information on institutional and governance structure was collected during country missions and through reports written by local consultants who are familiar with the institutional environment of each country. Evidence on coverage, distribution, and effectiveness of social spending comes primarily from several household surveys and sector-specific data collected by different line ministries and partners covering 2005–14. Appendix A lists the household surveys used in each country.[2]

Notes

1. For example, recent investigations and convictions of government officials in Guatemala for corruption make it politically difficult for the government to call for new taxes despite low levels of revenue and spending. In Costa Rica, because a large part of the government budget can be attributed to autonomous public institutions such as the utility and insurance companies, the legislature and executive have effective control over only less than half of public spending. In Costa Rica and Nicaragua, the constitution mandates spending on tertiary education.

2. We explore household surveys for the following years: Costa Rica (2007–14); El Salvador (2007–13); Guatemala (2006, 2011, and 2014); Honduras (2007–13); Nicaragua (2005, 2009, and 2014); and Panama (2007–13).

CHAPTER 2

Context: Progress and Opportunities for Human Development in Central America

The countries of Central America are relatively small in population, area, and size of economies. They have a common history and culture but in many ways are quite different from each other. For example, while Central American countries share many of the same human development problems, such as high secondary school dropout rates, challenges in providing health coverage to the entire population, large informal sectors, and inflexible and inefficient institutions and governance in the social sectors, there are both economic and noneconomic differences.

In economic terms, all Central American countries are middle income, but Nicaragua is the second-poorest country in Latin America and the Caribbean (LAC), after Haiti (World Bank 2015a). In noneconomic terms, El Salvador, Guatemala, Honduras, and Nicaragua have all had recent and violent civil conflicts, while Panama and Costa Rica have no armed forces. Especially in Guatemala, civil conflict has been related to a large population of indigenous peoples who often live in isolated rural communities and are excluded from the formal economy. Even though these conflicts ended in the 1990s, the aftermaths continue to exert a negative impact on human development. Youth and gang violence continues to be a serious public safety and human development issue in El Salvador, Guatemala, and Honduras, but not in Costa Rica, Nicaragua, or Panama. As a result, El Salvador, Guatemala, and Honduras are all among the top five countries in the world in terms of intentional homicide rates per capita (Honduras is number one).[1]

With the exception of Panama, economic growth in Central America has been slow. From 2007 to 2014, real average annual per capita gross domestic product (GDP) growth in Panama was 6 percent, compared to 2 percent in Costa Rica and Nicaragua, 1 percent in Guatemala and Honduras, and 0.75 percent in El Salvador (figure 2.1). Over the same period, the average annual per capita GDP growth rate in LAC overall was approximately 1.5 percent. The exceptional

Figure 2.1 GDP per Capita, 2000–14

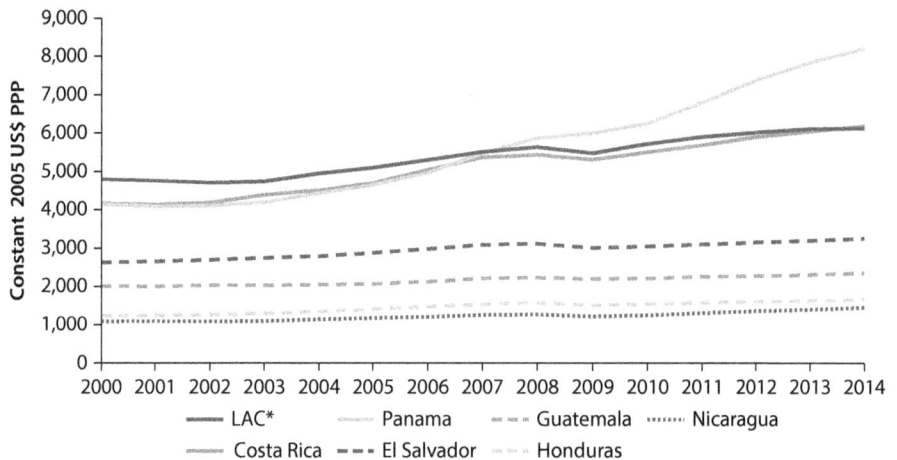

Source: World Bank 2015b, *World Development Indicators 2015.*
Note: LAC* aggregate consists of 17 countries in the region for which microdata are available at the national level.

growth performance in Panama stems primarily from the transfer of the Panama Canal to Panama in 1999, which allowed the country not only to benefit from the growth of world trade but also to leverage its geographic position to transform itself into a well-connected logistics and trade hub and a financial center (World Bank 2015a).

In recent years, Central America has achieved modest poverty reduction compared to the LAC average. Between 2007 and 2014, poverty rates declined more slowly in the subregion than in LAC as a whole (figure 2.2). The exception is Nicaragua, where poverty rates fell at a much faster rate than the LAC average. Poverty rates in Nicaragua fell from 59.2 percent in 2005 to 41.4 percent in 2014, while the average decrease in LAC over a similar period was approximately 9 percentage points. Progress in reducing poverty in Central America was slow in part because most Central American countries grew more slowly than the LAC average and because the economic growth that did occur had a smaller impact on poverty in Central America compared to the rest of Latin America. For example, despite being one of the most rapidly growing economies in the world, poverty in Panama fell by only 7.5 percentage points between 2008 and 2014. Within Central America, poverty fell in El Salvador, Nicaragua, and Panama, but increased in Guatemala and changed very little in Costa Rica and Honduras.

While poverty fell in Panama largely because of more rapid economic growth, poverty fell in El Salvador and Nicaragua due to a reduction in income inequality. Figure 2.3 presents changes in Gini coefficients between 2004 and 2014 and shows a fall in inequality in El Salvador and Nicaragua. World Bank estimates report that 100 percent of the fall in poverty in Panama between 2009 and 2014 was due to economic growth (with none of the fall due to redistribution) (World Bank 2016).

Figure 2.2 Poverty Rates, 2005–14

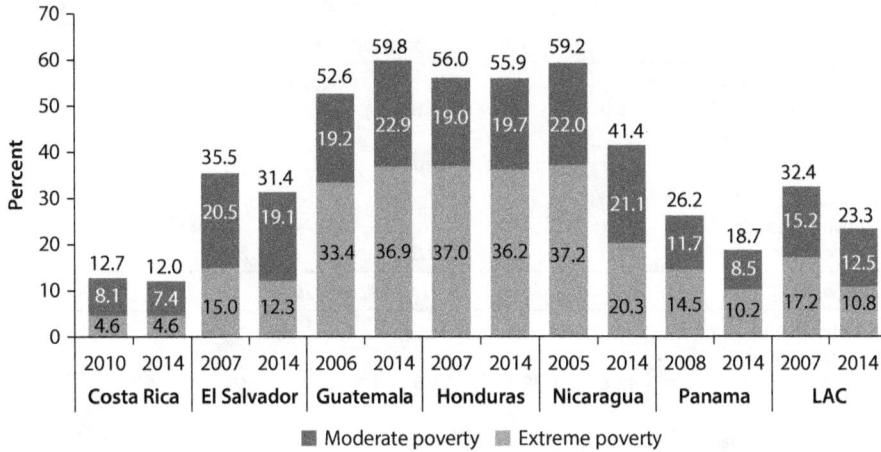

Source: World Bank calculations.
Note: Extreme poverty = US$2.50 a day, and overall poverty line = US$4 per day. The LAC aggregate consists of 17 countries in the region for which microdata are available at the national level.

Figure 2.3 Inequality (Gini Coefficient), 2004–14

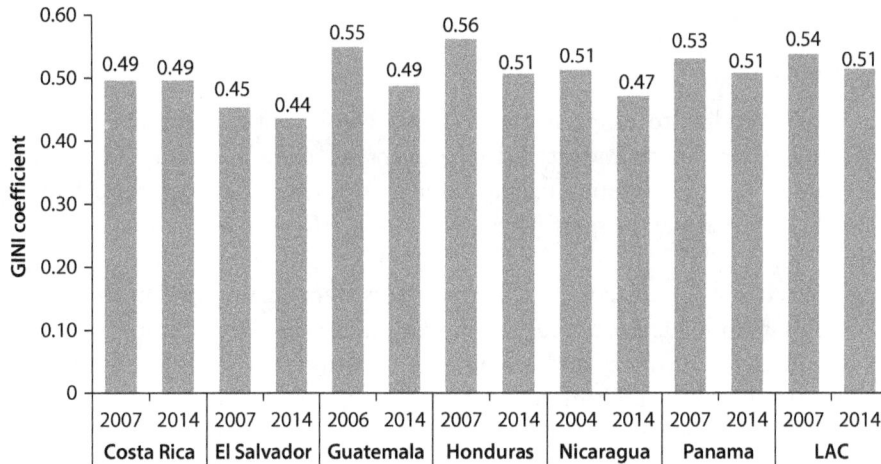

Source: World Bank 2015b, World Development Indicators 2015.

In contrast, World Bank estimates report that 100 percent of the fall in poverty in Nicaragua between 2009 and 2014 was due to redistribution, while in El Salvador more than 65 percent of the fall in poverty was due to redistribution (the rest was due to economic growth).[2]

There has been important progress in human development in Central America, but several common challenges persist across the region. Table 2.1 illustrates progress across the subregion, including increases in primary school

Table 2.1 Human Development Indicators, 2007–14

	CRI	SLV	GTM	HND	NIC	PAN	LAC
Progress	*Change in indicator, 2007–2014*						
Education: primary completion rate	5.0	9.5	10.8	2.5	3.9	7.5	2.0
Health: infant mortality rate	−0.4	−6.0	−8.4	−5.2	−5.0	−4.3	−3.5
Social protection and poverty: female labor force participation	1.6	2.5	1.8	2.4	2.7	1.7	1.9
Challenges	*Indicator, 2014*						
Education: secondary completion rate, 18–24 years old	42.7	38.2	19.5	32.1	33.0	54.2	N/A
Health: maternal mortality ratio per 100,000 live births	26.0	54.0	93.0	132.0	154.0	97.0	69.0
Social protection and poverty: 15–18-year-old NEETs	13.0	17.6	20.5	26.3	11.3	10.5	19.1

Sources: World Bank 2015b, *World Development Indicators 2015*; World Bank analysis of household surveys; and World Bank calculations using standardized ADePT software, the World Bank's software platform for automated economic analysis (Education Module).
Note: CRI = Costa Rica; GTM = Guatemala; HND = Honduras; NEETS = youth who are neither in school nor employed nor in training; NIC = Nicaragua; PAN = Panama.

enrollment leading to near-universal primary enrollment and graduation in all countries, infant mortality rates declining for all countries, and the average decrease in Central America falling faster than the LAC average, and female labor force participation rates higher than the LAC average (and rising in all countries).

As discussed in subsequent chapters, persistent challenges in almost all countries include high secondary school dropout rates; lack of improvements in the quality of primary and secondary education; a low share of students in higher education; high maternal mortality ratios; lack of adequate nutrition for many children; an aging population that will need increasing medical care for noncommunicable diseases; high rates of informality in the labor market; a large number of youth who are neither in school nor employed nor in training (NEETs); and severe inequalities by income, gender, region, and ethnic group.

Never before has the population of working-age people in Central America been so high, and never before has the dependency burden been so small. This demographic change has opened a window of opportunity where a small percentage of dependent young and old allows resources to be used to increase investments in education, health, and social protection, as well as physical capital. This window will close when the bulk of the current working-age population

Figure 2.4 Distribution of Youth, 15–18 Years Old, by Activity (2014 or Most Recent Year)

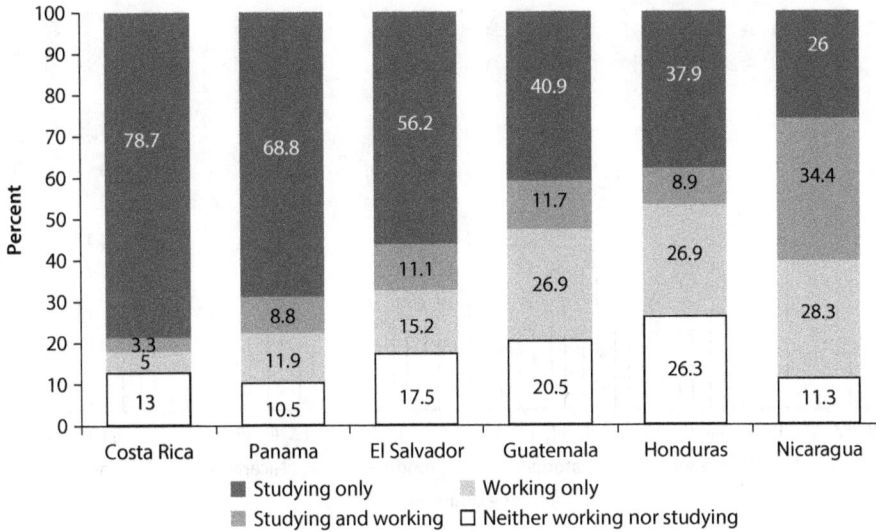

Legend:
■ Studying only   ▨ Working only
▨ Studying and working   ☐ Neither working nor studying

Source: ERCA 2016.

retires. If this chance is lost to improve the quality and coverage of public investments in human capital, it could have negative consequences for economic development well into the future.

More than two out of ten 15-to-18-year-olds in Central America are neither in school nor employed. The proportion of NEETs ranges from 10.5 percent in Panama and 11.3 percent in Nicaragua to 20.5 percent in Guatemala and 26.3 percent in Honduras (figure 2.4).[3] These figures compare to a Latin American average of 18.5 percent in 2009 (Cárdenas, de Hoyos, and Székely 2011). This socially excluded population represents a significant loss to the economy and society not only now, but predicts problems in the future. It illustrates the importance of addressing the problems of education coverage and quality, and of high youth unemployment, especially for children in the 15–18 age group.

Young people from low-income households are much more likely to neither study nor work. In all Central American countries, more than 30 percent of the proportion of children in the first quintile of the income distribution neither study nor work, compared to an average of 22 percent for the entire population of 15–18-year-olds (figure 2.5). Youth who neither study nor work are a heterogeneous group. The largest proportion of them are young women who live in rural areas and are engaged in unpaid domestic work (representing from 51.7 percent in Costa Rica to 84.6 percent in Guatemala) (PEN 2016).

Figure 2.5 Distribution of Youth, by Activity and Income Quintile (2012 or Most Recent Year)

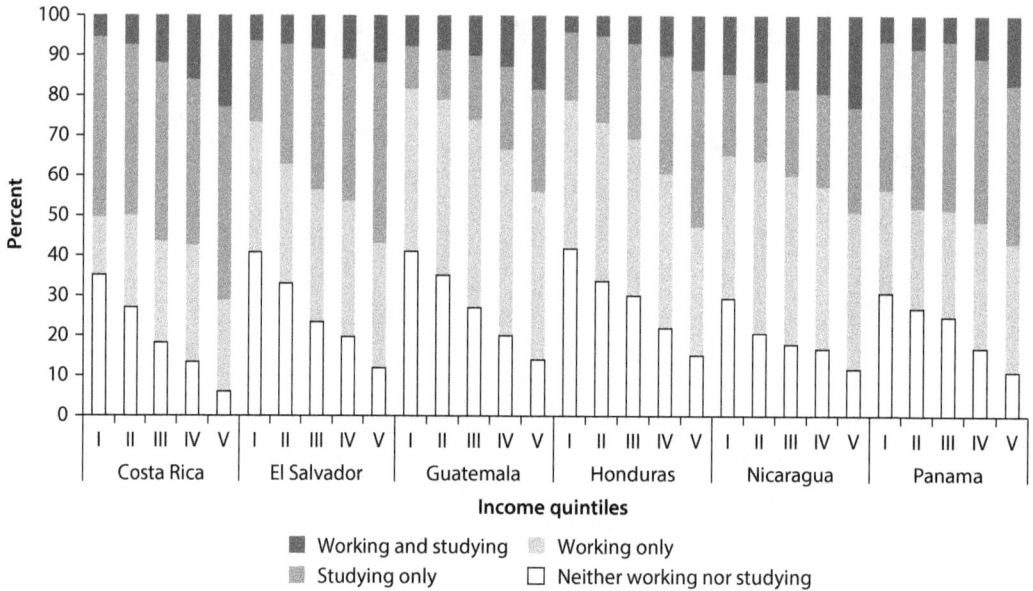

Source: PEN 2016.

Notes

1. United Nations Office on Drugs and Crime's International Homicide Statistics database.

2. World Bank (2016b) and Gindling, Thomas, and Trejos (2014) show that the biggest measureable reason for the fall in inequality in El Salvador and Nicaragua from 2000 to 2010 was a decline in returns to education.

3. Those who are 15–18 years old are much more likely to study full time in Costa Rica and Panama than in other Central American countries. About 79 percent of 18–25-year-olds are full-time students in Costa Rica, compared to 56 percent in El Salvador, 41 percent in Guatemala, 38 percent in Honduras, and 26 percent in Nicaragua. Nicaragua is unusual in the high proportion of young people who are both working and studying (34.4 percent of 15–18-year-olds). Adding those studying full time to those who work and study, the proportion of 15–18-year-olds who are students in Nicaragua is higher than in Guatemala and Honduras, but lower than El Salvador, Panama, and Costa Rica.

References

Cárdenas, M., R. de Hoyos, and M. Székely. 2011. *Idle Youth in Latin America: A Persistent Problem in a Decade of Prosperity*. Washington, DC: Brookings Institution.

ERCA (Programa Estado de la Región). 2016. "Quinto Informe Estado de la Region: El dilema estrategico de la educación en Centroamérica." Statistical Appendix. http://www.estadonacion.or.cr/erca2016/.

PEN (Programa Estado de la Nación). 2016. "Mejorar la educación: dilema estratégico para el desarrollo de Centroamérica." Quinto informe Estado de la Nación, Quito.

World Bank. 2015a. *Panama—Country Partnership Framework for the Period FY15–FY21.* Washington, DC: World Bank.

———. 2015b. *World Development Indicators 2015.* Washington, DC: World Bank.

———. 2016. *Poverty and Shared Prosperity at a Glance.* Washington, DC: World Bank.

CHAPTER 3

Recent Trends in Social Spending across the Region and Sectors, 2007–14

As a percentage of gross domestic product (GDP), between 2007 and 2014 public social spending increased in Costa Rica, El Salvador, Nicaragua, and Guatemala but fell in Honduras and Panama. Two countries (Costa Rica and Honduras) had higher shares of public spending relative to GDP compared to the average for Latin America and the Caribbean (LAC) (figure 3.1). In 2014, El Salvador, Nicaragua, and Panama had public social spending to GDP levels similar to the LAC average. In Panama, the fall in social spending as a percentage of GDP may be misleading because it masks an increase in real per capita social spending along with a dramatic increase in GDP. Although Guatemala's social spending share of GDP increased, it is still only about half the LAC average (figure 3.1).

Overall per capita social spending levels in Central America are low compared to other countries in LAC and compared to other countries with similar per capita GDP, except for Costa Rica, where it is much higher. The next highest, Panama, spends less than one-third that of Costa Rica and is similar to El Salvador, a country with a much lower GDP per capita. The lowest levels of social spending per capita are in Guatemala. Even in Costa Rica, social spending per capita is lower than other Latin American countries with similar GDP per capita such as Argentina, Trinidad and Tobago, Uruguay, Chile, and Brazil (figure 3.2).

In most Central American countries, the share of the budget spent is less than 100 percent of that allocated. Budget execution in 2013 ranged from 85 percent in Honduras to 95 percent in El Salvador (figure 3.3). Budget execution in El Salvador is not only high but increasing (92 percent in 2007 to 94 percent in 2013). Budget execution in Honduras was high (99 percent) in 2007 but fell substantially between 2007 and 2013 (to 85 percent), especially in education.[1] Honduras and Panama had the lowest budget execution rates in 2013/2014, at 85 percent and 88 percent respectively. Next come Costa Rica and Guatemala

Figure 3.1 Social Expenditure as a Share of GDP, 2007–14

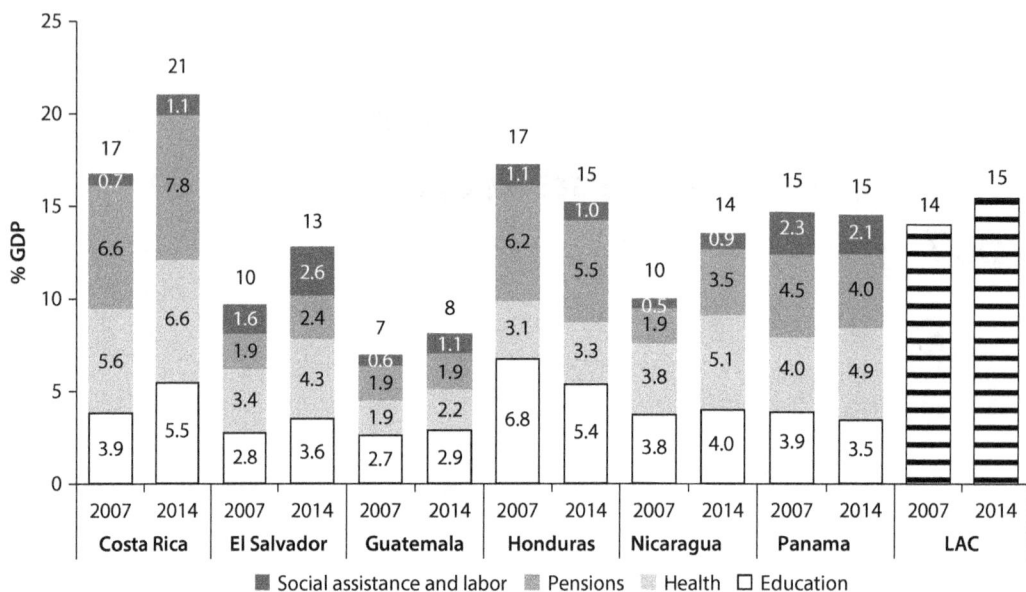

Legend: Social assistance and labor ▪ Pensions ▪ Health ☐ Education

Sources: World Bank SSEIR/ICEFI social spending database. LAC figure is from CEPAL.

Figure 3.2 Per Capita Social Public Expenditure, by Sector, 2012 or Latest Year Available

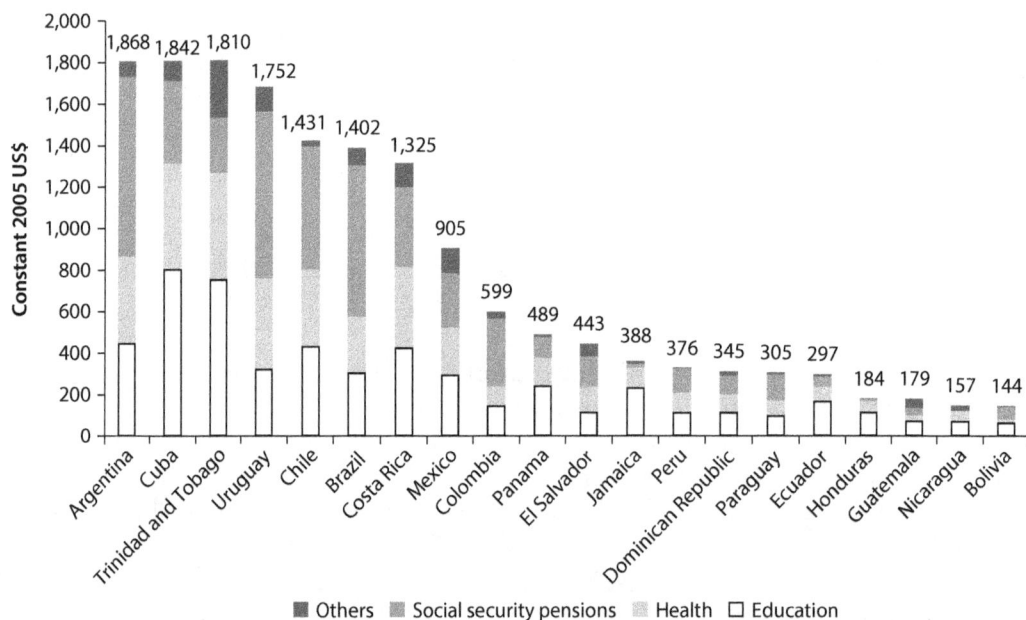

Legend: ▪ Others ▪ Social security pensions ▪ Health ☐ Education

Source: CEPAL.

Figure 3.3 Budget Execution, by Sector, 2007–14

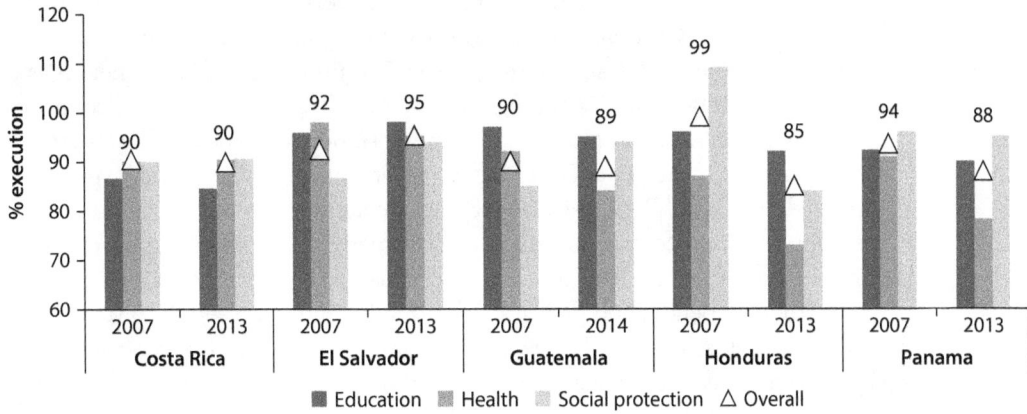

Source: World Bank SSEIR/ICEFI social spending database.

with budget execution rates of 90 percent and 89 percent, respectively, in 2013/2014, suggesting that despite a high and increasing level of social spending in Costa Rica, there is still room for improvement in implementation efficiency, while with respect to Guatemala, this underscores the need to address implementation bottlenecks. Budget execution fell in Panama between 2007 and 2013 (from 94 percent to 88 percent), especially in health, primarily because of decreases in the capital budget execution rates for both the Ministry of Health (MOH) and the Social Security Institute. Combined with rapid GDP growth, this suggests that Panama faces capacity constraints in executing its planned capital investments in the health sector.

The distribution of social spending differs among countries. As a percentage of total public spending, social spending is the largest in Nicaragua and Guatemala, followed by Panama, Costa Rica, Honduras, and El Salvador. Social security pension spending is the largest part of social spending in Costa Rica and Honduras (reaching 14 percent and 13 percent of total public spending in Costa Rica and Honduras, respectively, in 2014). Health and education spending is a big part of social spending in each country. Public spending on health ranged from 2.2 percent of GDP in Guatemala to 6.6 percent in Costa Rica in 2014 (figure 3.1).

Education spending is highest in Costa Rica (5.5 percent of GDP in 2014) and Honduras (5.4 percent in 2014) and falls to 4 percent in Nicaragua, 3.5 percent in Panama, 3.6 percent in El Salvador, and 2.9 percent in Guatemala (figure 3.1). SPL is the smallest part of social spending (less than 2.7 percent of GDP in all countries in 2014) but is increasing as a percentage of GDP in all countries except Panama (figure 3.1; although because of rapid GDP growth, real per capita social protection and labor (SPL) spending is also rising in Panama).

Between 2007 and 2014, social spending as a percentage of total public spending increased in Costa Rica, Guatemala, and Nicaragua, while it fell in the other Central American countries. As a percentage of GDP, education spending increased in all Central American countries between 2007 and 2014, with the largest increase in Costa Rica (from 3.9 percent of GDP in 2007 to 5.5 percent in 2014). Between 2007 and 2014, the share of public spending on health as a percentage of total public spending increased in all Central American countries except in El Salvador and Honduras (figure 3.4). Between 2007 and 2014, social security as a percentage of GDP, and as a percentage of total public spending, increased in Costa Rica, Nicaragua, and Guatemala, while social assistance spending as a percentage of total public spending increased in all Central American countries except Honduras and Panama (figures 3.1 and 3.4).

Per student spending on primary education is similar to the LAC average and other countries at similar GDP per capita (figure 3.5). Except for Panama, spending on primary education is the largest component of public education spending in all Central American countries. In all Central American countries except Honduras, per student spending on secondary education is less than the LAC average and other countries at similar levels of development. On average, per student spending on secondary education in Central America is US$9.58, less than the LAC average of US$15.49 (figure 3.6). In Panama, spending on tertiary education is greater than on primary or secondary education (figure 3.7).

Between 2007 and 2014, public education spending increased in Costa Rica and El Salvador, both as a percentage of GDP (from 3.9 percent of GDP to 5.5 percent in Costa Rica and 3 percent to 3.6 percent in El Salvador) and in real per capita terms (by 13.2 percent in Costa Rica and 4.4 percent in El Salvador).

Figure 3.4 Social Spending as a Share of Total Public Spending in the Subregion, 2007–14

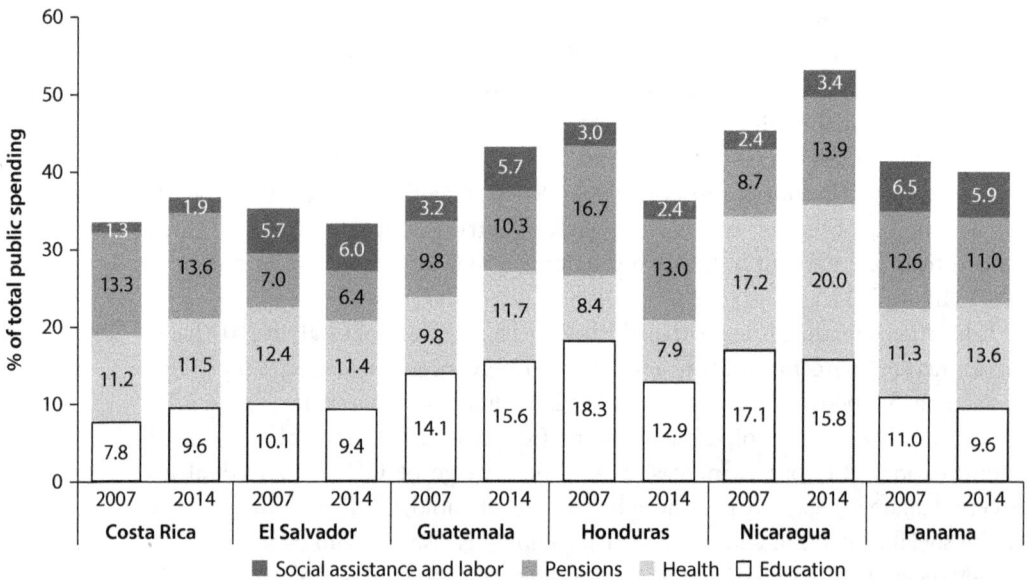

Source: ICEFI.

Figure 3.5　Primary Public Expenditure per Pupil as a Share of GDP per Capita Compared with GDP per Capita

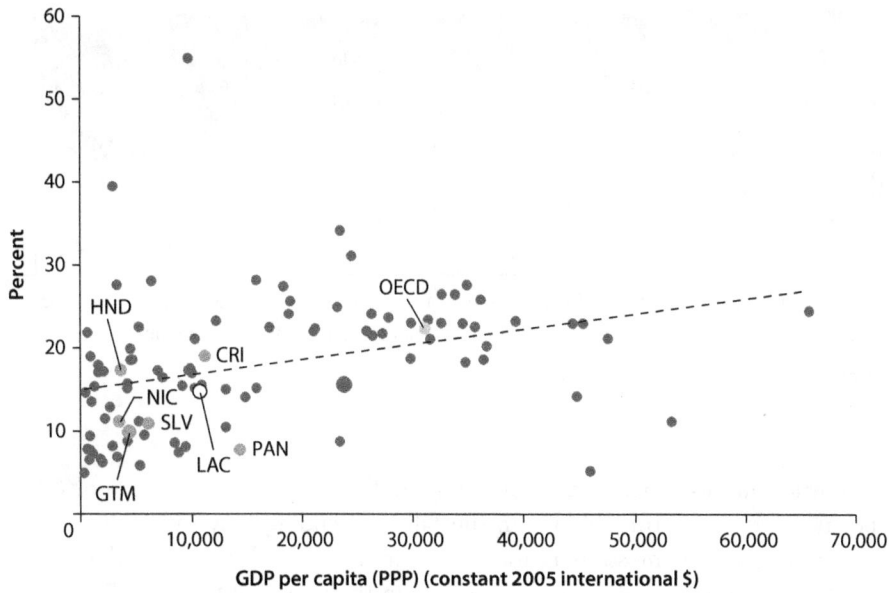

Source: World Bank 2015, *World Development Indicators 2015.*
Note: CRI = Costa Rica; GTM = Guatemala; HND = Honduras; NIC = Nicaragua; OECD = Organisation for Economic Co-operation and Development; PAN = Panama; PPP = purchasing power parity; SLV = El Salvador.

Figure 3.6　Secondary Public Expenditure per Pupil as a Share of GDP per Capita Compared with GDP per Capita

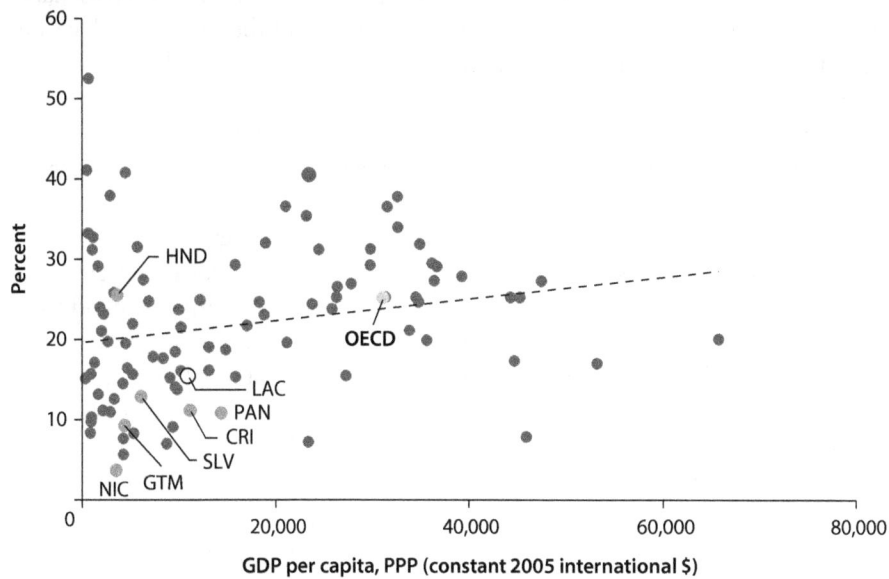

Source: World Bank 2015, *World Development Indicators 2015.*
Note: CRI = Costa Rica; GTM = Guatemala; HND = Honduras; NIC = Nicaragua; OECD = Organisation for Economic Co-operation and Development; PAN = Panama; PPP = purchasing power parity; SLV = El Salvador.

Toward More Efficient and Effective Public Social Spending in Central America
http://dx.doi.org/10.1596/978-1-4648-1060-2

Figure 3.7 Public Spending, by Educational Level, as a Share of Education Public Spending in the Subregion, 2014

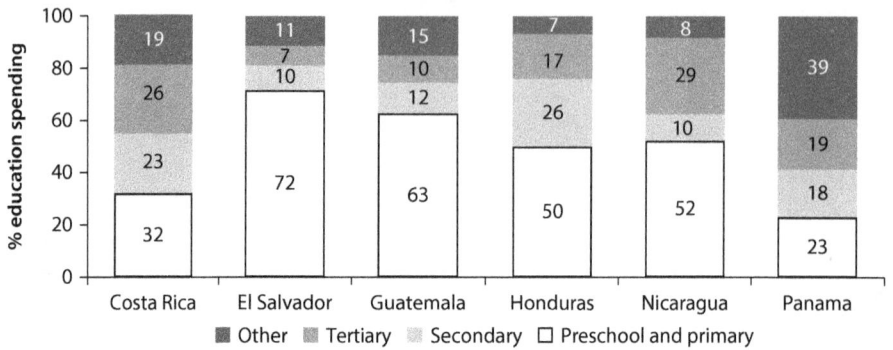

Source: World Bank SSEIR/ICEFI social spending database.

In contrast, in Honduras, education spending fell both as a percentage of GDP and in per capita terms. However, the fall in spending may overestimate the decline in government support for education. As we will see later, this fall in spending in Honduras was due to a decline in the wage bill from 2007 to 2013 after historic highs in 2007 (due to historically high teacher salaries). In Guatemala and Nicaragua, because of slow economic growth, education spending increased as a percentage of GDP but fell in real per capita terms.

In all Central American countries except Panama, spending on preschools and primary schools is the largest part of education spending, ranging from 72 percent of education spending in El Salvador to 32 percent in Costa Rica. This is reasonable given that more students are enrolled in primary school than in higher levels of education. One exception is Panama simply because of the size of the spending on group "others," at 39 percent of education spending, while spending on preschool and primary is only 23 percent. Spending on tertiary education is highest in Nicaragua (29 percent) and Costa Rica (26 percent) and is as low as 7 percent in El Salvador (figure 3.7).

In Panama, education spending increased in per capita terms between 2007 and 2014 by 30.2 percent but fell as a percentage of GDP, from 3.9 percent to 3.4 percent. Excluding "Other" (including other administrative expenditures like the "Beca Universal" scholarship[2]), education spending decreases across all educational levels. The "other" category increased at an annual average rate of 2 percent from 2007 to 2013. Public spending in preschool education as a percentage of GDP decreased from 0.12 percent in 2007 to 0.09 percent in 2013. During the same period, spending in primary education as a percentage of GDP decreased by 0.26 percentage points, in secondary education by 0.30 percentage points, and in tertiary education by 0.24 percentage points. Unfortunately, because the spending data we explore did not fully allocate the spending in "Other" by education level, it is impossible to quantify these levels by educational level very accurately.[3]

Throughout Central America, despite increases in total spending on education and despite increased enrollments in the first years of secondary school, public spending on secondary education has been stable or falling in recent years. Between 2007 and 2014, public spending on lower secondary increased substantially only in Guatemala and was stable in every other country (figures 3.8 and 3.9). From 2007 to 2014, public spending on upper secondary increased substantially only in Costa Rica, and was stable or falling in every other country (figure 3.10).

Public spending on health as a percentage of GDP increased in all Central American countries between 2007 and 2014. It increased the most in

Figure 3.8 Preprimary and Primary Public Education Spending in the Subregion, 2007–14

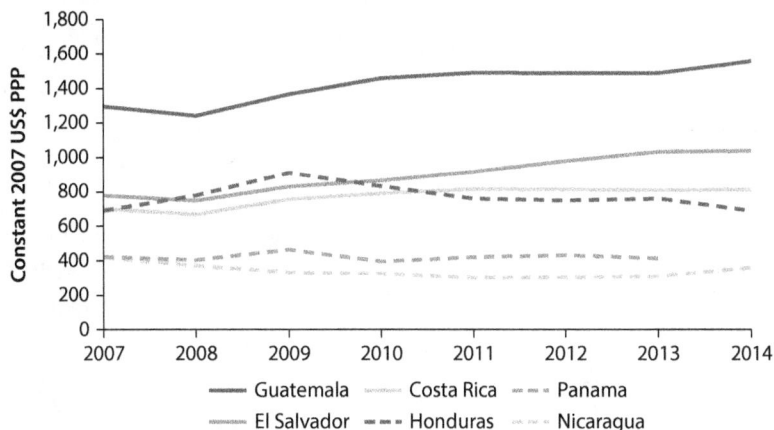

Source: World Bank SSEIR/ICEFI social spending database.

Figure 3.9 Lower Secondary Public Spending, 2007–14

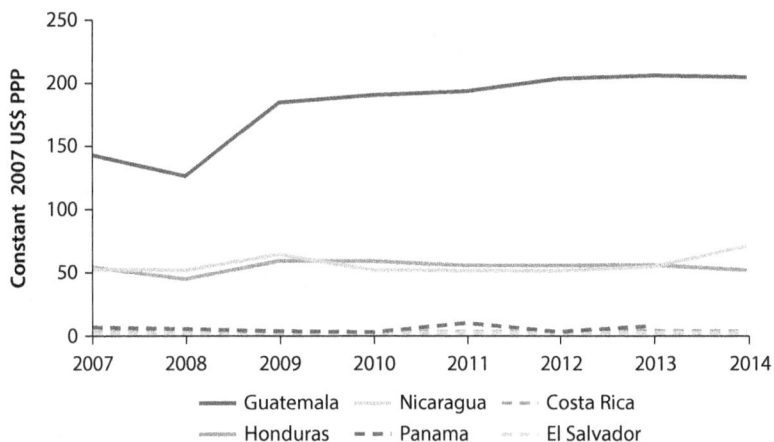

Source: World Bank SSEIR/ICEFI social spending database.

Toward More Efficient and Effective Public Social Spending in Central America
http://dx.doi.org/10.1596/978-1-4648-1060-2

Figure 3.10 Upper Secondary Public Spending, 2007–14

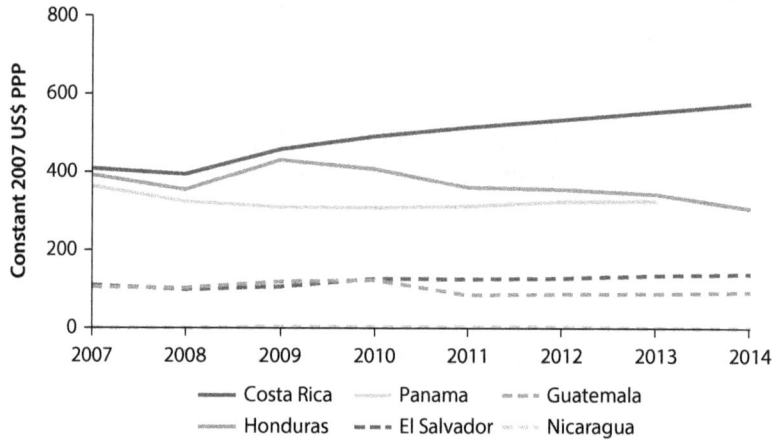

Source: World Bank SSEIR/ICEFI social spending database.

Nicaragua (33 percent), followed by El Salvador (20 percent) and Costa Rica (17 percent) during this period (figure 3.11). Nevertheless, except for Costa Rica and Nicaragua, public spending on health as a percentage of GDP is low compared to the LAC average and to other countries with similar GDP per capita (figure 3.12). Public spending on health is particularly high in Costa Rica, where it is similar to the OECD country average as a percentage of GDP (figure 3.12).

Panama has the highest real per capita public spending on health in Central America, followed by Costa Rica and El Salvador. Real per capita public spending on health is lowest in Guatemala, Honduras, and Nicaragua (figure 3.13). Panama's real per capita health public spending is at least twice that of El Salvador and five times more than Guatemala, Honduras, and Nicaragua. Real per capita public spending on health increased significantly in Panama between 2007 and 2014 (figure 3.13).

Hospitals and salaries account for the largest share of public expenditure in health in most countries in Central America. Hospitals comprised the largest share of expenditures among health programs in five[4] Central American countries (figure 3.14). Panama and Honduras allocated a much higher share of public spending on health to hospitals (65 percent and 58 percent, respectively) than the LAC average (49 percent). Although Guatemala's public spending share on hospitals is almost in line with the LAC average, its hospitals still face frequent shortages of equipment and supplies. While Nicaragua allocated the largest share of its expenditures to hospitals (45 percent), it spent almost the same share on primary health care (PHC) services (43 percent). In terms of spending categories, salaries accounted for the largest share of expenditures in all countries in Central America (figure 3.15). Except for Nicaragua, the countries allocated a higher share of total public spending on health (at least 60 percent) to wages compared to the average for middle-income countries (52.5 percent).

Figure 3.11 Public Spending on Health as a Share of GDP, 2007–14

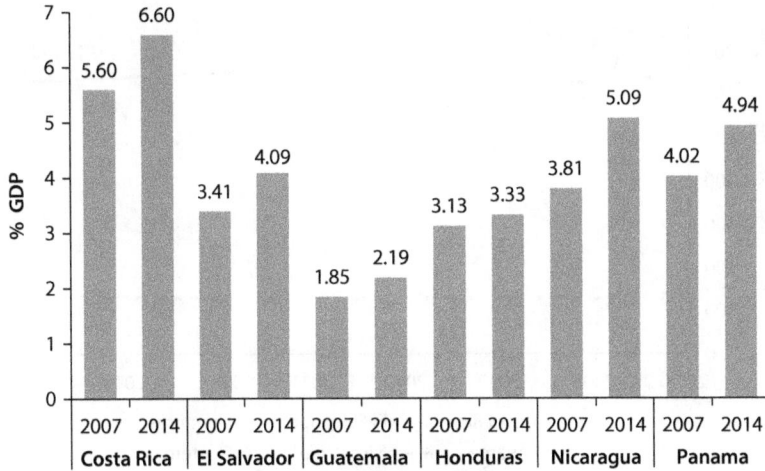

Source: World Bank SSEIR/ICEFI social spending database.

Figure 3.12 Public Expenditure on Health as a Share of GDP Compared with GDP per Capita, 2013

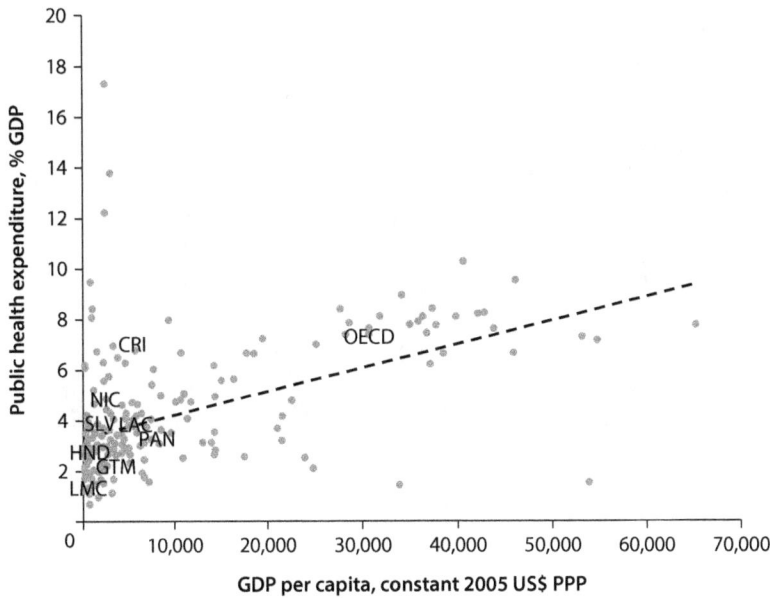

Source: World Bank 2015, *World Development Indicators 2015.*
Note: CRI = Costa Rica; GTM = Guatemala; HND = Honduras; LMC = lower-middle-income-country average; NIC = Nicaragua; PAN = Panama; SLV = El Salvador.

Public spending in SPL has grown significantly since 2007 both in real per capita terms and as a share of GDP in the majority of Central American countries. SPL spending as a share of GDP grew on average 9 percent per year in Nicaragua (rising from 2.4 percent of GDP in 2007 to 4.4 percent in 2014), 6 percent in El Salvador, and 3 percent in Costa Rica and Guatemala, and

Figure 3.13 Per Capita Public Spending on Health

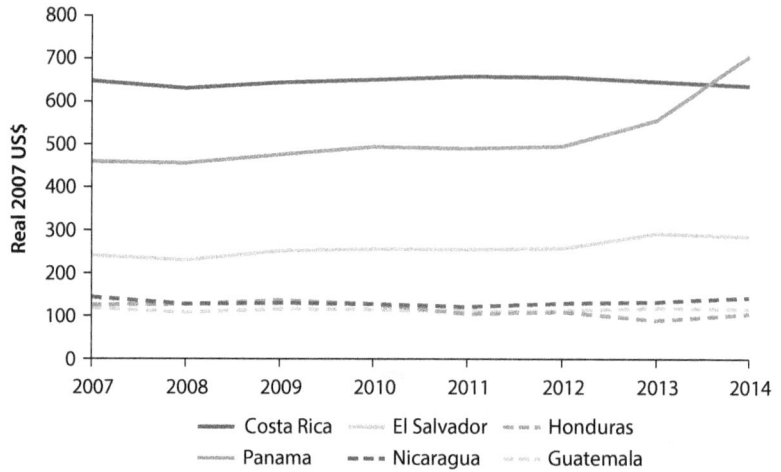

Source: World Bank SSEIR/ICEFI social spending database.

Figure 3.14 Share of Hospitals in Public Spending on Health

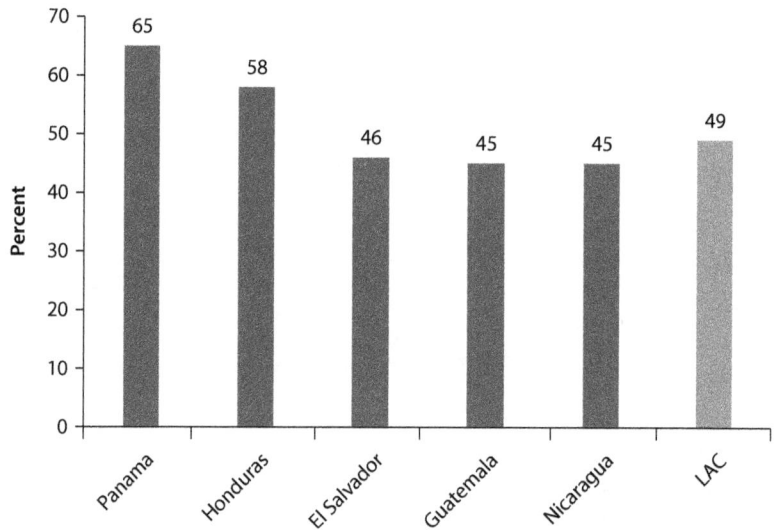

Source: World Bank SSEIR/ICEFI social spending database. Costa Rica disaggregated spending not available.

decreased 1 percent per year in Honduras and Panama, albeit from a high level (figure 3.16). In per capita terms, SPL spending also rose in real terms during that same period in all countries except Honduras, with an average of US$425 per capita in the subregion in 2014 (figure 3.17). Still, this masks important dispari-ties across countries, since per capita spending ranges from around US$865 to US$880 per capita in Costa Rica and Panama to US$125 to US$160 in Nicaragua and Guatemala.

Figure 3.15 Share of Public Spending on Health Spent on Salaries

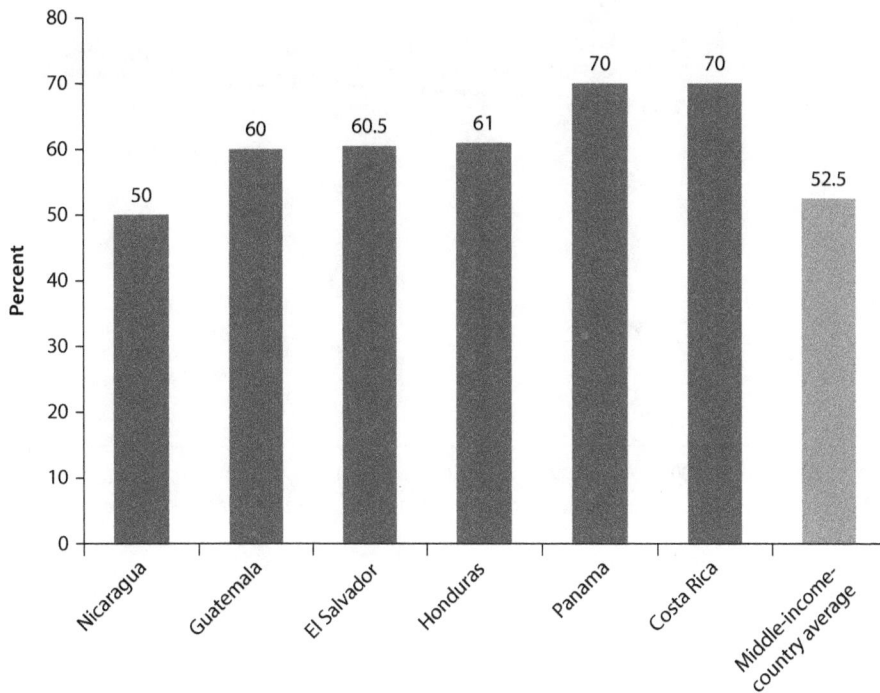

Sources: MOH-Ministry of Finance Guatemala 2014, Honduras 2011, El Salvador 2012. Middle-income-country average share from Clements et al. 2010.
Note: Honduras, Guatemala, El Salvador, and Nicaragua are shares of MOH spending and Panama and Costa Rica are shares of total public spending on health (2010).

Figure 3.16 SPL Spending as a Share of GDP, by Country

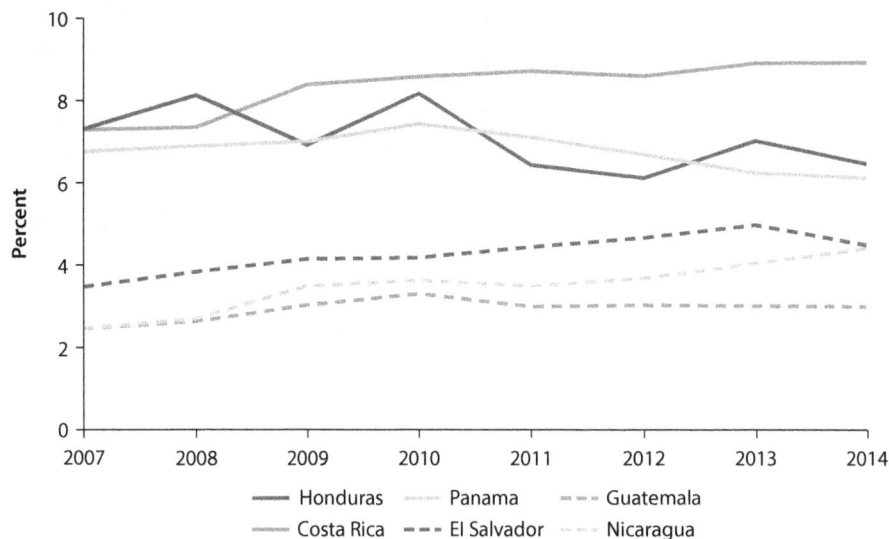

Source: World Bank SSEIR/ICEFI social spending database.

Toward More Efficient and Effective Public Social Spending in Central America
http://dx.doi.org/10.1596/978-1-4648-1060-2

Figure 3.17 SPL Spending per Capita, by Country

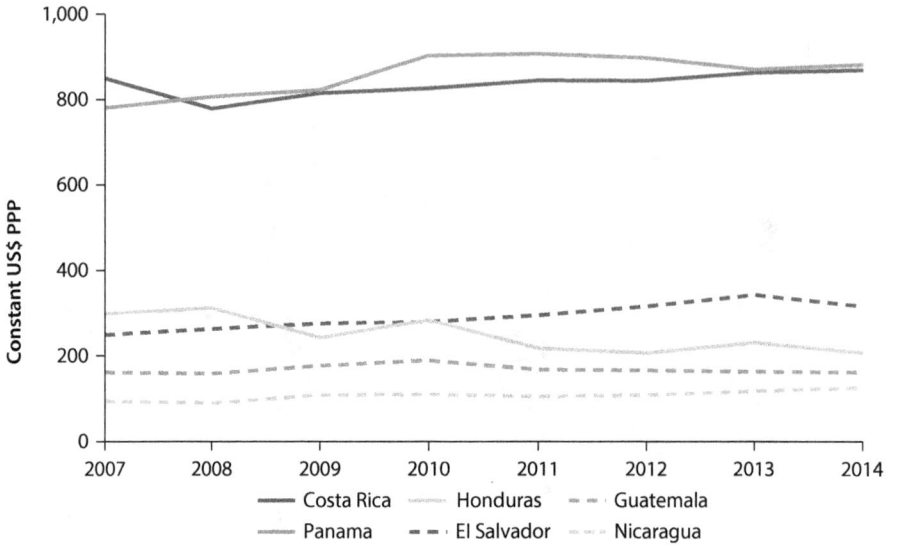

Source: World Bank SSEIR/ICEFI social spending database.

The largest part of public spending on SPL is social security pensions. As a percentage of GDP, public spending on pensions is highest in Costa Rica (8.7 percent), which has one of the most generous pension programs in LAC. Social security pension spending (only accounting for contributory schemes) is lowest in Guatemala (3.0 percent) (figure 3.18). Pensions may be contributory or noncontributory. Contributory pensions are paid to those who contributed to social security while working. Those workers are mostly in the formal sector, and the pension payments increase with contributions.

Subsidies and CCTs account for the largest part of social assistance spending. Regressive untargeted subsidies account for the majority of social assistance and labor spending in El Salvador (1.3 percent of GDP in 2014) and a relatively large fraction of spending in Panama (0.6 percent) and Guatemala (0.3 percent). Cash transfers (which are progressive) are a big percentage of social assistance spending only in Costa Rica and Honduras, an important but smaller percentage of social assistance spending in El Salvador and Panama, and a very low percentage in Guatemala and Nicaragua. The percentage of GDP spent on cash transfers equals 0.6 percent in Costa Rica and Honduras, 0.3 percent in El Salvador and Panama, 0.1 percent in Guatemala, and is negligible in Nicaragua. Overall average spending in active labor market programs (ALMPs) is 0.3 percent of GDP, about half the average in OECD countries (0.6 percent of GDP). Only in Costa Rica and Nicaragua is spending on ALMPS important and near the OECD country average as a percentage of GDP (figure 3.18).

Figure 3.18 Social Assistance and Labor Spending as a Share of GDP, 2014

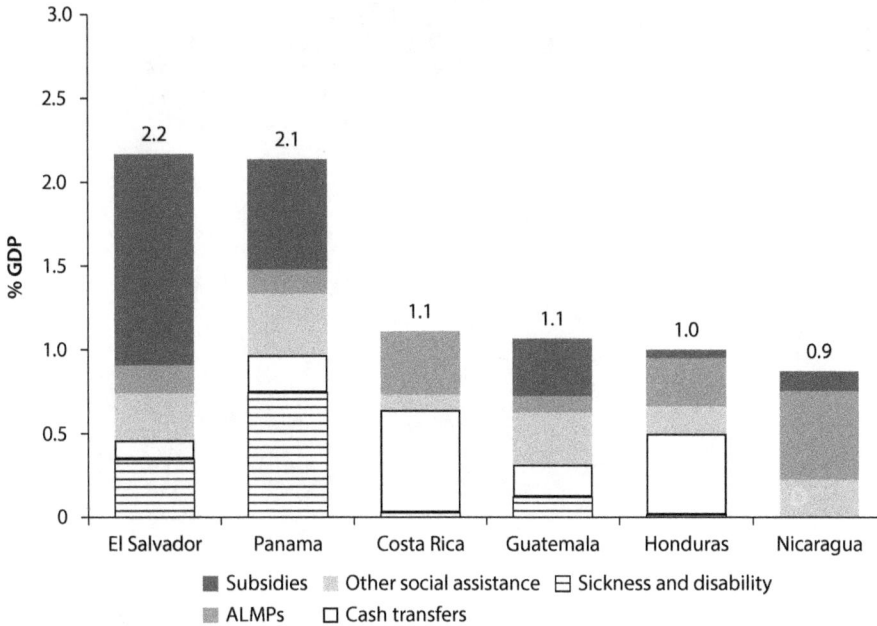

Source: World Bank SSEIR/ICEFI social spending database.

Notes

1. More than any other Central American country, the wage bill is a very large part of education spending in Honduras, and 2007 was a year when teacher salaries were highest. As a percentage of education spending, wages and the wage bill fell by 2013. Low and falling levels of social spending in Honduras suggests that Honduras needs to increase the levels and efficiency of social spending.

2. Beca Universal" (Universal Scholarship) is a major educational initiative of the Panamanian government to improve educational outcomes and retention (see World Bank 2015). Student-focused and performance-based, this cash scholarship encompasses all educational levels and regions to provide more than 600,000 payments a year for 180,000 eligible children with a total budget of US$125M.

3. Scholarships are distributed in many categories inside the public spending in education, but the biggest share is in "other," specifically in spending in education not definable by level.

4. Costa Rica did not have data disaggregated by health programs because of its health system's integrated approach to care.

References

Clements, B., S. Gupta, I. Karpowicz, and S. Tareq. 2010. *Evaluating Government Employment and Compensation.* Washington, DC: International Monetary Fund.

World Bank. 2015. *World Development Indicators 2015.* Washington, DC: World Bank.

CHAPTER 4

Coverage and Targeting

Education Coverage and Targeting

The overall structure of the educational systems in all Central American countries is similar, with six years of formal primary schooling, three years of lower secondary, and three years of upper secondary, plus preprimary and tertiary. Students enter primary school grade 1 at age 6 in Costa Rica, El Salvador, Honduras, and Panama and at age seven in Guatemala and Nicaragua. In all countries of the subregion, public primary and secondary schools are free. In all countries except Nicaragua, education from primary through lower secondary is compulsory. In Nicaragua, upper secondary and one year of preprimary are also compulsory. Tertiary education typically includes academic and technical colleges and universities.

All countries in the subregion have achieved near-universal primary coverage rates and have made significant gains in preprimary and secondary enrollment, but gaps in access remain in preprimary and secondary levels across all countries. All Central American countries have very high primary school enrollment and completion rates. Figures 4.1 and 4.2 show that net enrollment rates are always above 80 percent, ranging from 86 percent in Guatemala to 98 percent in Costa Rica. Dropout rates in primary school have also fallen in almost all Central American counties in the past decade. Gross enrollment rates in lower and upper secondary have increased in all countries, with substantial increases in lower and upper secondary gross enrollment in Costa Rica and Panama and large increases in lower secondary enrollment in El Salvador.

However, even in these countries, many students still drop out before completing upper secondary (see figure 4.1 and 4.6). Dropout rates in lower secondary are relatively low in Costa Rica (23 percent), Panama (25 percent), and El Salvador (27 percent), while lower secondary dropout rates are higher in Guatemala (37 percent), Honduras (42 percent), and Nicaragua (43 percent). The pattern for upper secondary dropout rates is the opposite, with higher upper secondary dropout rates in Costa Rica (53 percent), El Salvador (55 percent),

Figure 4.1 Gross Enrollment Rates across All School Levels in the Subregion, 2007–14

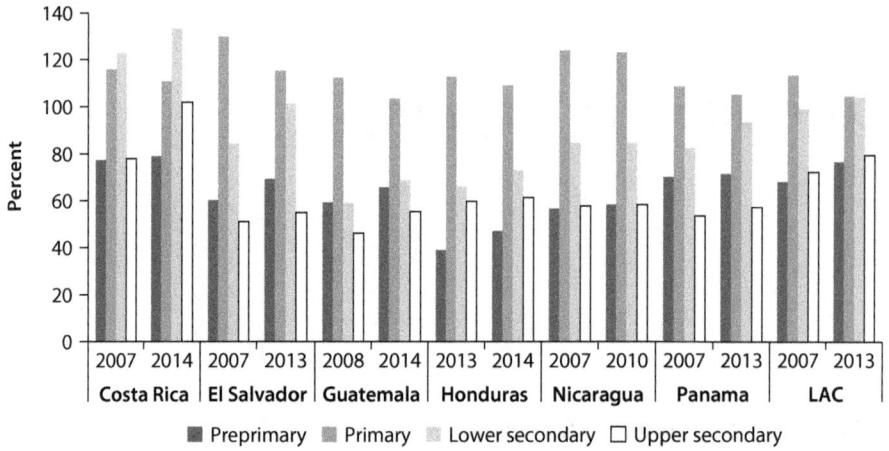

Sources: EdStats; UNESCO Institute for Statistics; 2014 or latest data available.

Figure 4.2 Net Enrollment Rates across All School Levels in the Subregion, 2007–14

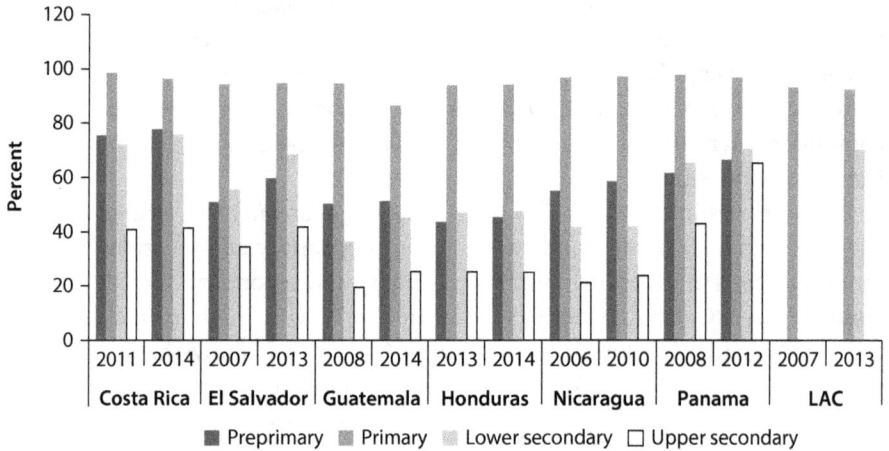

Sources: EdStats; UNESCO Institute for Statistics; 2014 or latest data available.

and Panama (57 percent) compared to Guatemala (42 percent), Honduras (39 percent), and Nicaragua (34 percent) (Adelman and Szekely 2016, reporting dropout rates for 2014 or for the most recent year).

Between 2007 and 2014, there was progress in Central America in improving access to preprimary education; however, in all countries enrollments are still far from universal. For instance, from 2007 to 2014 gross and net enrollment rates for preschool increased in all countries of the subregion (figures 4.1 and 4.2). Honduras, in particular, had a rapid increase, where the net enrollment rate in preprimary increased from 43 percent to 54 percent. The next-fastest growth in preprimary enrollment was in El Salvador. By 2014, the highest preprimary net enrollment rates were in Costa Rica, which had high preprimary enrollment rates in 2007 but relatively little growth between 2007 and 2014. The lowest net preprimary enrollment rates are in Guatemala, which also experienced very little growth between 2007 and 2014 (figures 4.1 and 4.2).[1] This is critical, because the access to high-quality preprimary education in developing cognitive and noncognitive skills in later years has been well established in the literature, especially for developing countries (Berlinski and Schady 2015).

Furthermore, there are also large differentials in daycare and preschool attendance within countries across regions and income quintiles, which are further compound by large differences in quality. The findings show that low-income families have less access to preprimary education. For example, figure 4.3 shows the shares of preschool attendance in Costa Rica, which range from 27 percent of children in the first income quintile to 49 percent in the top income quintile. Furthermore, when designed and implemented well, there is well-established evidence that high-quality early childhood development programs act as equalizers, since they can reduce the effect of household socioeconomic differences on the child's cognitive and noncognitive development and, therefore, the ability to perform well in school (Chetty, Friedman, and Rocko 2014).

Especially in rural areas, where population density is lower and there are more challenges in the provision of formal preschools, there is also a need for high-quality parenting programs to support early cognitive and socioemotional development of children to get them school ready. For instance, figure 4.4 shows that the number of students enrolled in preschool is larger in urban areas than in rural areas in Nicaragua. Further, more students in rural areas are in "community preschools" than "state" or "formal preschools." As noted in the next paragraph, community preschools in the subregion, tend to still face several challenges both in terms of the quality of the learning environment and the training of the caregivers, one good example is Nicaragua.

In Nicaragua, community preschools are usually led by "volunteers" (or *educadoras comunitarias*), who only receive a small formal payment from the state

Figure 4.3 Costa Rica Daycare and Preschool Attendance, by Income Quintile, 2014

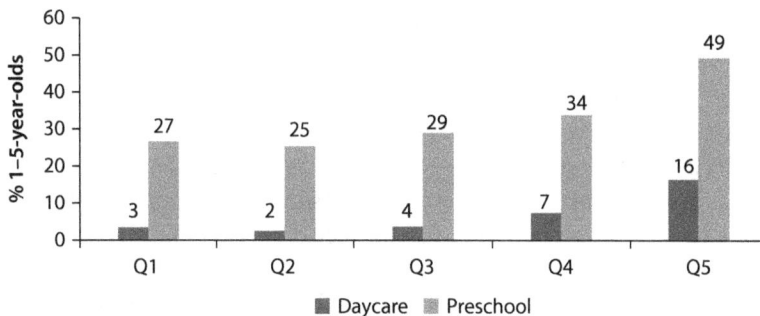

Sources: World Bank analysis of household surveys and staff calculations using standardized ADePT software (Education Module).

Figure 4.4 Preschool Enrollment, by Type, State Compared with Community, Nicaragua, 2009

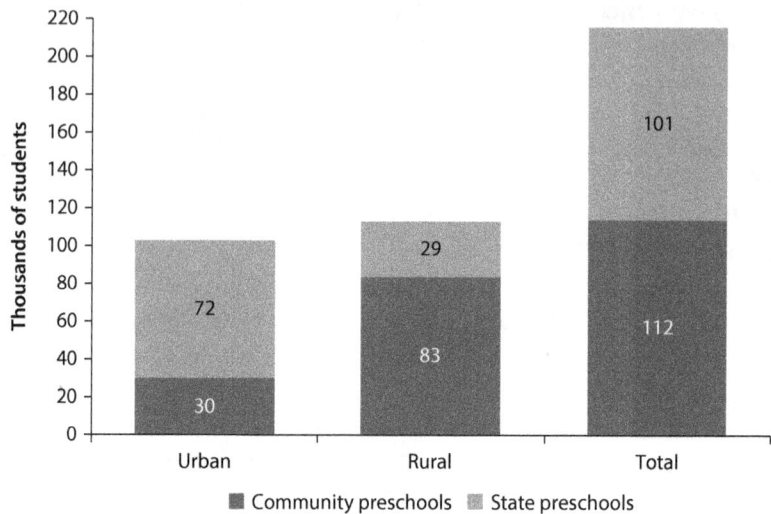

Source: World Bank using Ministry of Education information (2009).

(*aporte voluntario*). The *educadoras comunitarias* are, in most cases, young girls from the communities who work as volunteers. They are located on private property, usually from religious organizations, or in unused houses, with minimal security standards, borrowed by community members. School furniture tends to be provided by community members, and learning materials are not systematically provided by the state. The average monthly salary of formal basic education teachers is much higher than the salary of community preschool teachers (figure 4.5).

The new Quality Model for Preschool Education is a recent policy effort to improve access to, and quality of, preschools. In 2011, the government began an important effort to increase access to formal preschools in rural areas, with new preschool classrooms in rural primary public schools. In addition, it also launched the Quality Model for Preschool Education, which is: Setting the same quality standards for both formal and community preschools, and second, (ii) Following a community-centric approach, involving parents and local authorities in preschool activities, such as the preparation of school meals.[2]

Enrollment rates in the first year of lower secondary education tend to be high in the subregion, but many students drop out before completing lower secondary in Guatemala, Honduras, and Nicaragua. In Costa Rica, El Salvador, and Panama, enrollment in the first year of upper secondary is high, but a significant number of students drop out before completing upper secondary (figure 4.6). All Central American countries except Honduras have had success improving enrollment rates in lower secondary during the past decade (figures 4.1 and 4.2). Costa Rica and El Salvador have also improved enrollment rates in upper secondary, although they remain low compared to other Latin American countries. "Thus, for Costa Rica, Panama and El Salvador upper secondary dropouts are clearly a

Figure 4.5 Teacher Salaries, by Level (National Currency, 2014)

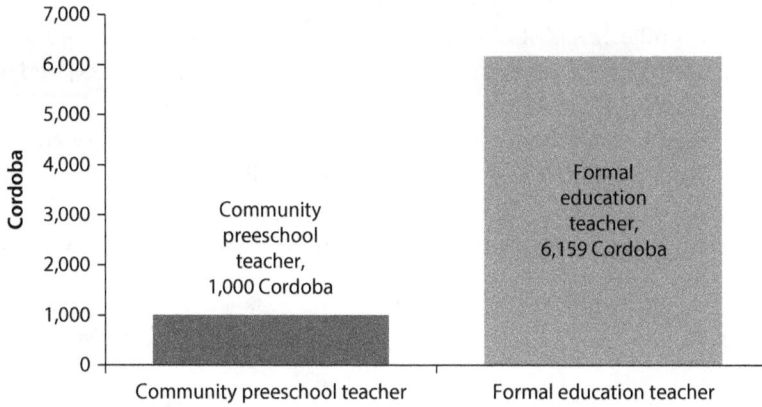

Source: World Bank staff using Ministry of Education information (2009).

Figure 4.6 Lower Enrollment Rates after Primary School, Ages 5–20

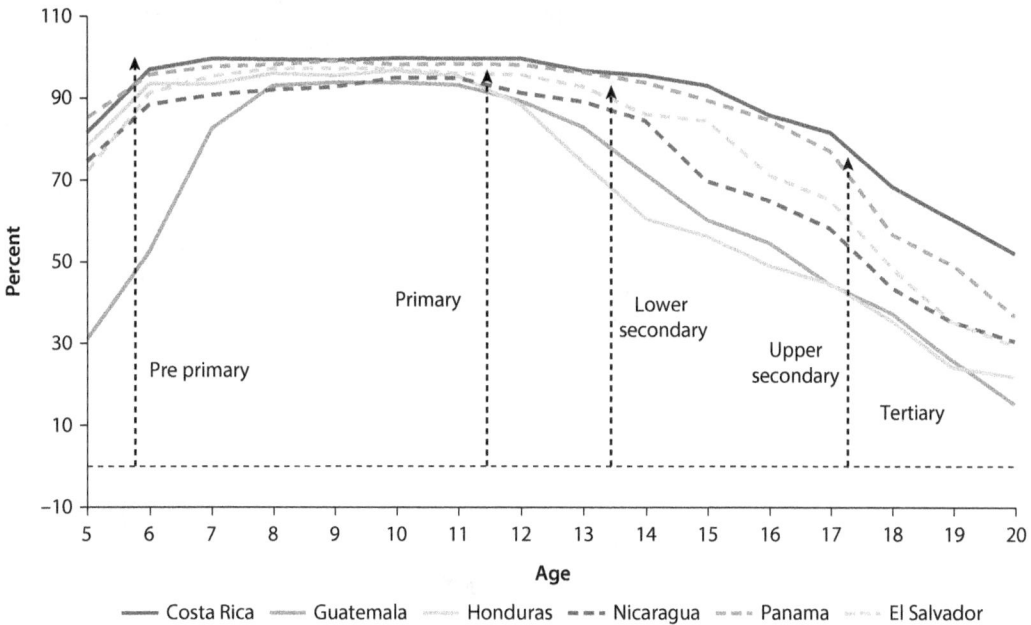

Sources: World Bank staff analysis of household surveys and staff calculations using standardized ADePT software (Education Module).

central challenge. Guatemala Honduras and Nicaragua also face this challenge, but additionally, they are still struggling with the issue of lower secondary completion" (Adelman and Szekely 2016, 8).

High dropout rates at the secondary level result in the low educational attainment in Central America. Except for Costa Rica and Panama, average years of education are lower in Central America than in other countries at similar levels of development (figure 4.7). In particular, secondary dropout rates are high, and secondary completion rates are low in all Central American countries compared to the Latin America and the Caribbean (LAC) average and other countries at similar levels of development (figure 4.8). High secondary dropout rates are a particular problem because secondary education is considered a prerequisite for access to good jobs that bring families out of poverty (PEN 2016). In addition, because a secondary degree is a prerequisite for tertiary education, secondary dropout contributes to low tertiary enrollment.

Figure 4.7 Average Years of Total Schooling (25+) Compared with GNI per Capita

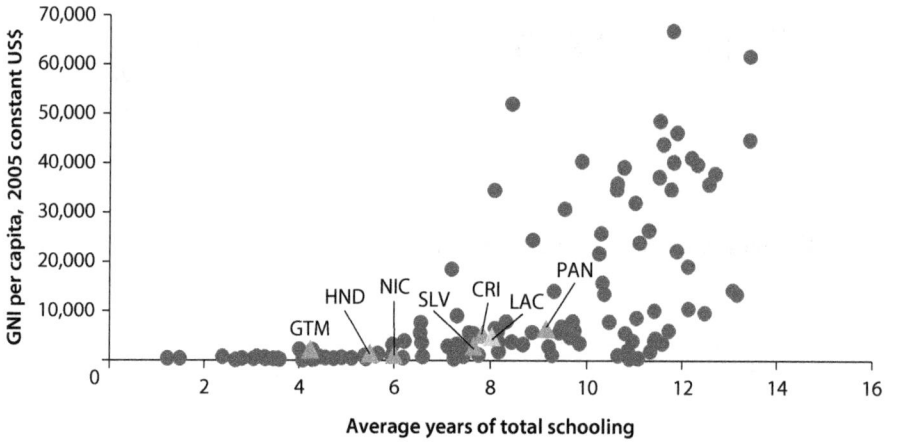

Source: Edstats, World Bank.
Note: CRI = Costa Rica; GTM = Guatemala; HND = Honduras; LA = Latin America; NIC = Nicaragua; PAN = Panama; SLV = El Salvador.

Figure 4.8 Secondary Completion Rate, Ages 25+

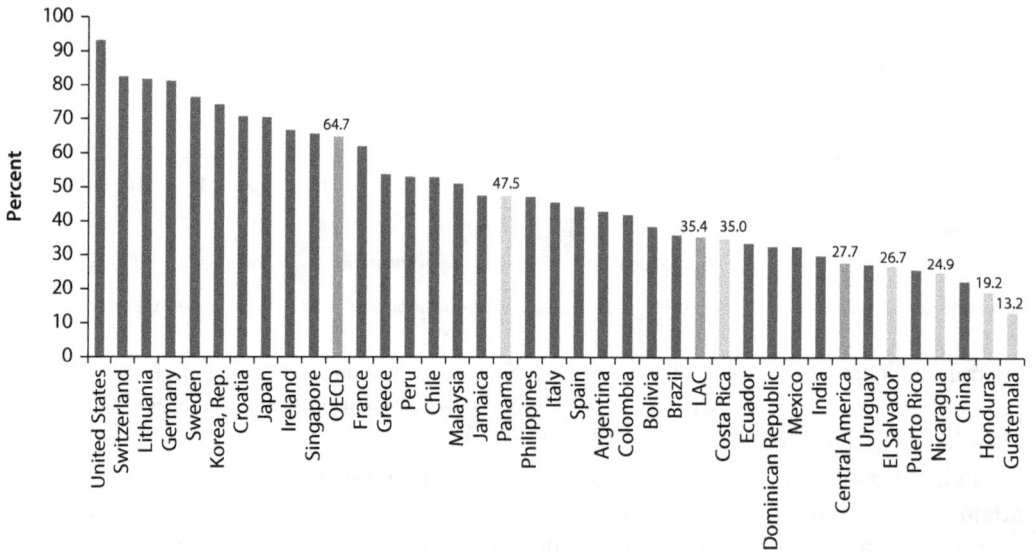

Source: EdStats, World Bank.

Dropout rates are particularly high for rural schools, indigenous regions, and those in low-income households. The largest gaps in enrollment rates for 12–17-year-olds in Costa Rica, Panama, El Salvador, and Guatemala are between youth in the richest and poorest quintiles and between urban and rural schools (figure 4.9). Enrollment and dropout rates in primary and lower secondary are not that different for girls and boys.

Throughout the region, low-quality public education pushes those who can afford it to private education. Only the wealthiest students can afford private secondary schools, which generally have more and better inputs (figure 4.12). The flight of the wealthy to private schools, especially at the secondary level, is likely due to the higher inputs and outcomes in these schools compared to public schools (figure 4.13). As a result, a large fraction of children belonging to the wealthiest families are sent to private schools. In El Salvador, only 4 percent of those in the first quintile of the income distribution attend private schools, compared to 54 percent in the top quintile. Public opinion polls in El Salvador show little belief that public education has improved in recent years. In Costa Rica and Guatemala, only 1 percent of those in the first quintile attend private secondary schools, as do 5 percent in Honduras. Thirty-five percent of those in the top quintile in Costa Rica and Honduras attend private secondary schools, as do 71 percent in Guatemala.

Students in urban areas are also much more likely to attend private schools than are those in rural areas (figures 4.10 and 4.11). In Guatemala, children from wealthier households also attend private schools, especially at the beginning of the secondary level (figure 4.11). According to the 2011 Encuesta Nacional de Condiciones de Vida (National Survey of Life Conditions; ENCOVI), wealthier households enroll in private schools at a much higher rate than poor households do. While only 1 percent of the poorest quintile of households enroll students in private primary schools, 29 percent of students from the wealthiest household

Figure 4.9 Enrollment, by Location, Indigenous Regions, and Income Distribution, Ages 5–20, 2013

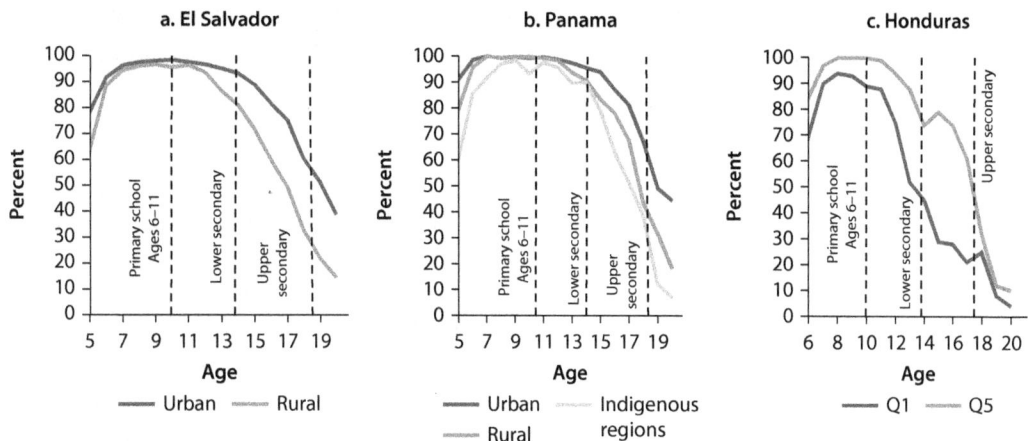

Sources: World Bank analysis of household surveys; calculations using standardized ADePT software (Education Module).

Toward More Efficient and Effective Public Social Spending in Central America
http://dx.doi.org/10.1596/978-1-4648-1060-2

Figure 4.10 Youth Attendance Rates, by Type of School, Location, and Income Quintile, Ages 13–18, Honduras, 2013

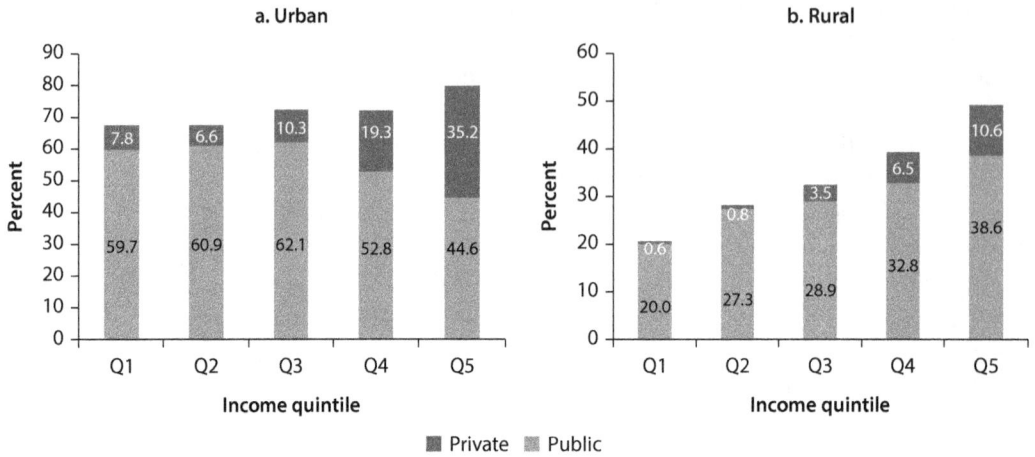

a. Urban

b. Rural

Sources: World Bank analysis of household surveys; calculations using standardized ADePT software.

Figure 4.11 Public and Private Enrollment, by Income Quintile, Guatemala, 2014

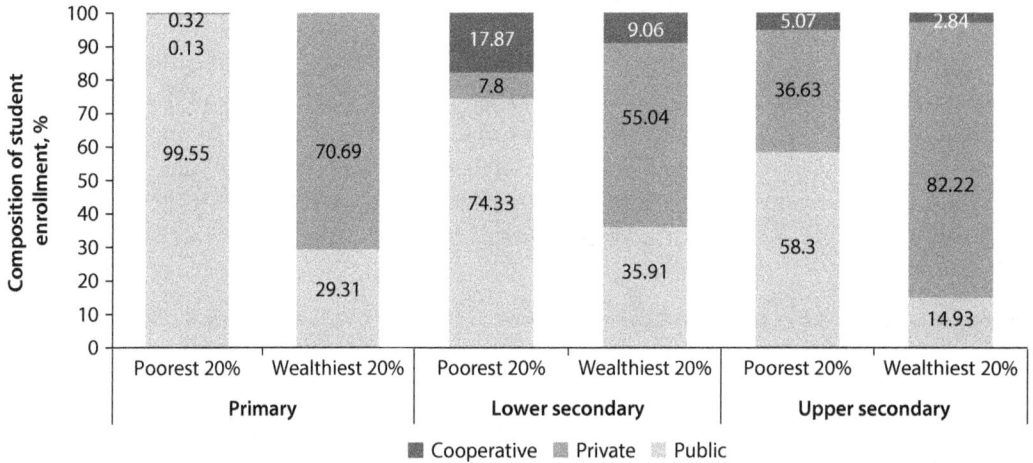

Source: World Bank analysis of ENCOVI 2011 data; calculations based on ADePT software.

quintile are in private school. Wealthy households can choose between public schools and high-cost private schools, which often have better facilities and more qualified teachers than public schools and in turn may have better learning and completion outcomes. Poor households often have to choose between public schools and low-cost private schools, which can have worse outcomes than public schools. While wealthy households may choose between public and private options based on quality, the poorest households (often in rural areas) may be forced to choose based simply on availability of spaces.

Figure 4.12 Share of 15–19-Year-Olds Attending Private School, by Income Quintile, Costa Rica, 2014

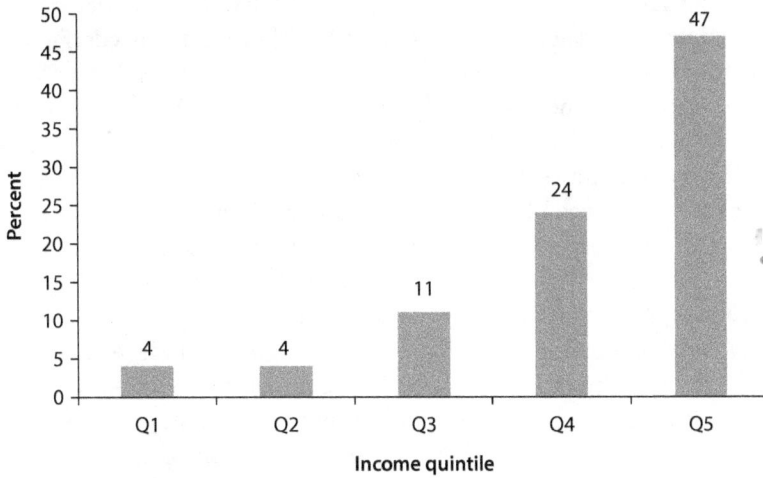

Sources: World Bank analysis of household surveys; calculations using National Household Survey (2013).

Figure 4.13 Computers per Student in Public and Private Schools, Costa Rica

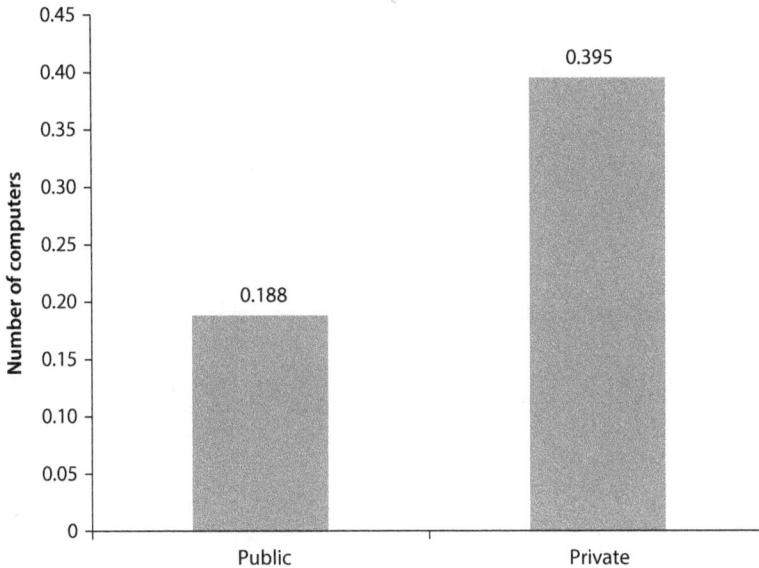

Sources: World Bank analysis of household surveys; calculations using National Household Survey (2013).

Anecdotal evidence suggests that "demand-side" problems that contribute to higher dropout rates in Central America include low family income, lack of interest, teen pregnancy, violence, gangs, and single-parent households. Young people report that the two most important reasons for dropping out are lack of money (liquidity constraints) and lack of interest (figure 4.14).[3] Economic causes (lack

Toward More Efficient and Effective Public Social Spending in Central America
http://dx.doi.org/10.1596/978-1-4648-1060-2

of money and working) are the most important reasons for dropping out before completing upper secondary in Guatemala and Honduras, while lack of interest is most important in Costa Rica and Nicaragua. Lack of interest may be because the curriculum is outdated and does not reflect labor market needs. Figure 4.15 presents the reasons for dropping out of secondary school, separately for lower and upper secondary. The reasons differ in some respects. Work is a more important reason for dropping out in upper secondary than in lower secondary. Transportation difficulties (including distance to school) appear to be more important for lower secondary school than upper secondary.

Boys are more likely to report economic causes as a reason for dropping out of upper secondary, while girls are more likely to report personal and family reasons. Both girls and boys report lack of interest as an important cause of dropping out (figure 4.16). Family reasons for girls include teen pregnancy, single-parent households, and housework. Teen pregnancy discourages school attendance because it increases the opportunity cost of staying in school. For example, 5 percent of girls in Nicaragua and 11 percent of girls in Costa Rica listed pregnancy as a reason for dropping out. Adelman and Szekely (2016) also find that teenage pregnancy rates are high in Central America and that teen mothers face social pressure to stay home to take care of children, and lack the needed support to stay in school. One econometric study found that neighborhood violence levels are the best predictor of difficulties in school, especially for boys. Higher homicide rates lead to higher dropout rates in Guatemala, higher rates of grade repetition, and lower rates of promotion out of grade in all Central American countries (ERCA 2016). Gang violence is a particular problem for students in low-income regions and neighborhoods (Adelman and Szekely 2016).

Figure 4.14 Reasons for Dropping out of School, by Reason Reported

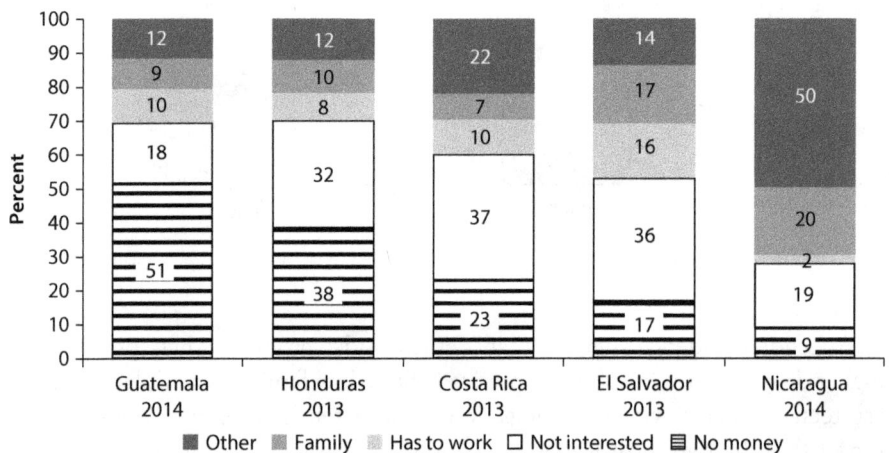

Source: World Bank calculations based on analysis of household surveys.

Figure 4.15 Reasons for Not Attending Secondary School, by Educational Level, 2014

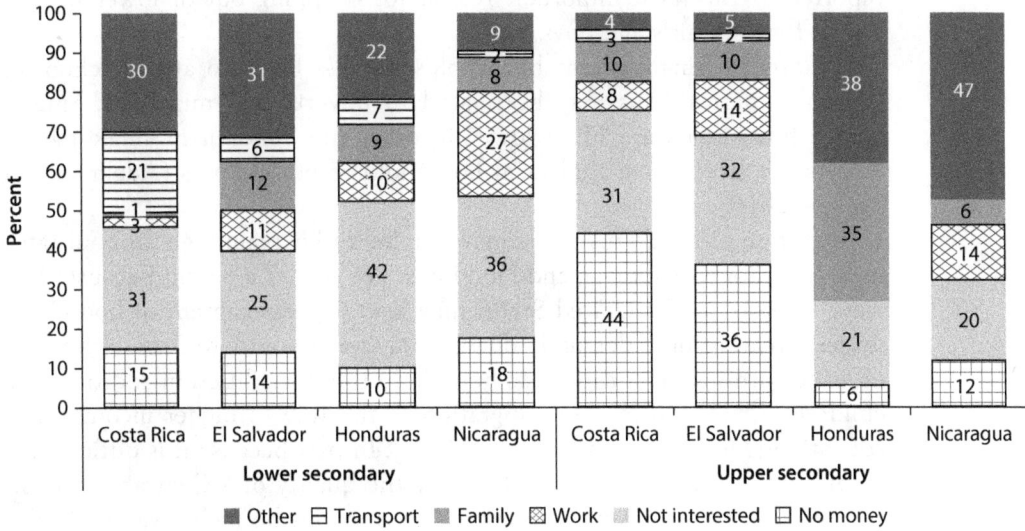

Source: World Bank calculations based on analysis of household surveys.

Figure 4.16 Reasons for Not Attending Upper Secondary School, by Gender, 2014

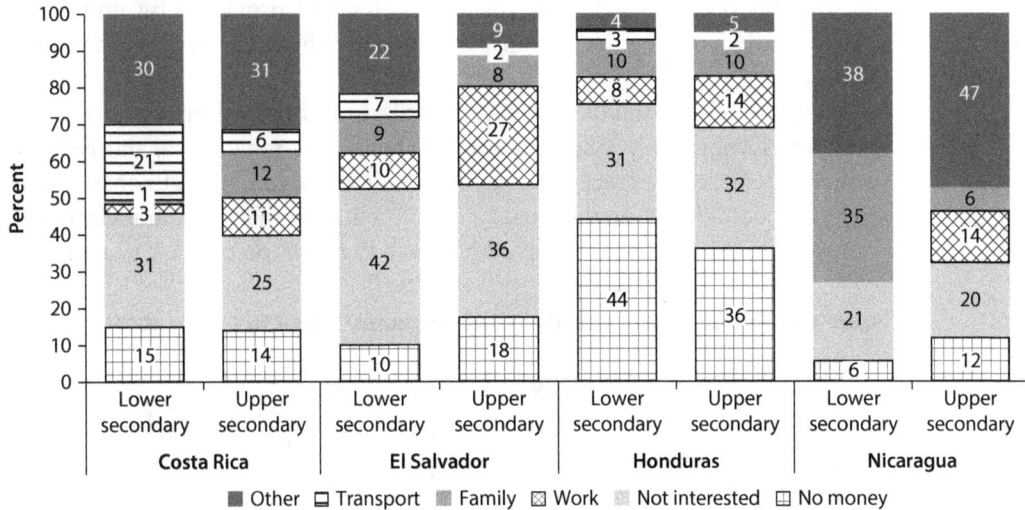

Source: World Bank calculations based on analysis of household surveys.

Lack of money and family reasons are the most important reasons that girls drop out of lower secondary in Honduras and Nicaragua, where lower secondary dropouts are a significant problem. About 46 percent of girls report family reasons as the cause of dropping out in Nicaragua, while 46 percent of girls (and 42 percent of boys) report lack of money as a reason for dropping out in Honduras (figure 4.17). In Costa Rica and El Salvador, where lower secondary dropout rates are not as big a problem, lack of interest is reported as the most important reason for dropping out of lower middle school for both girls and boys.

Children in single-parent households are less likely to attend school in Central America. This may be related to poverty and migration. Single-parent households are often lower income, and children in single-parent households likely have additional household responsibilities (Adelman and Szekely 2016).

Migration of family members may also help to explain high dropout rates in El Salvador, Guatemala, and Honduras. The loss of a parent because they leave to work in the United States may lead to reassignment of household duties, creating new demands on secondary-age youth to leave school in order to earn income or increase household responsibilities. In addition, the children left behind may see migration as the way to higher incomes, not education (McKenzie and Rapoport 2006). In part because it is difficult for employers in the United States to know the quality of a Central American education, a Central American education may not be highly valued in the United States, further enhancing the perception that returns to migration are higher than returns to education, which reduces demand for education in Central America. Central American immigrants in the U.S. are often employed in jobs below their education levels (Hall et al. 2011). Lack of information on the quality of the education and providers by employers abroad may be one of the reasons for reduced schooling investments in the subregion.[4]

"Supply-side" constraints that may contribute to higher dropout rates at the secondary level include long distance to school, high school fees, and reduced quality of education. Perceptions about quality, elicited by Latinobarómetro, show low confidence in the quality of schooling in many Central American countries. In El Salvador, for example, less than 30 percent of respondents

Figure 4.17 Reasons for Not Attending Lower Secondary School, by Gender, 2014

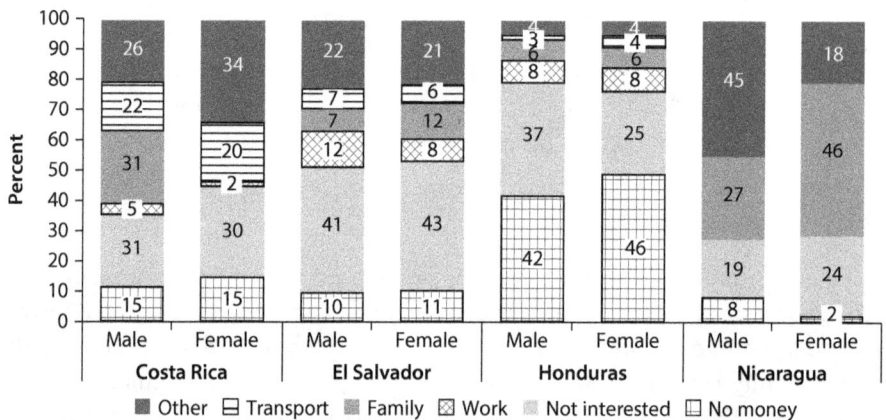

Source: World Bank calculations based on analysis of household surveys.

perceived improvements in the quality of the public education system in the 10 years before the survey.

Another indication of the prevalence of low-quality public secondary schools is the large percentage of students in private secondary schools. In all countries, most students are in public primary schools, but the proportion falls in secondary schools. In some countries, the majority of upper secondary students are in private schools. In Guatemala, for example, 91 percent of primary students attend public schools, while 56 percent of lower secondary schools do, and only 27 percent of upper secondary students attend public schools. A high quality of education is key for improving coverage; potential students are more likely to drop out if the quality of teaching and pedagogies is low.

Access (that is, distance to school) is a particular problem for students from rural communities because while primary schools are generally within walking distance of home, secondary schools often require transportation and possibly even living outside of the home (figure 4.18). Adelman and Szekely (2016) find that in most Central American countries, living in rural areas where distance to school is likely to be large (especially for indigenous peoples) has a bigger negative impact on enrollment in Central America than gender, parental background, and household size. To serve the entire out-of-school rural population in Honduras, the number of rural schools would need to be increased from 192 to 1,079.

Clearly there are also important links between the quality of pre-school and primary education quality. If students are not prepared for secondary school in primary, then they are more likely to drop out in secondary. Thus, low quality primary education may also be a reason for secondary drop outs, especially among the large group who report lack of interest as their reason for dropping out.

More comprehensive and diverse strategies accounting for the actual differences in the reasons for dropping out across and within countries are necessary.

Figure 4.18 Reasons for Not Attending School, Children Ages 13–18, Nicaragua, 2014

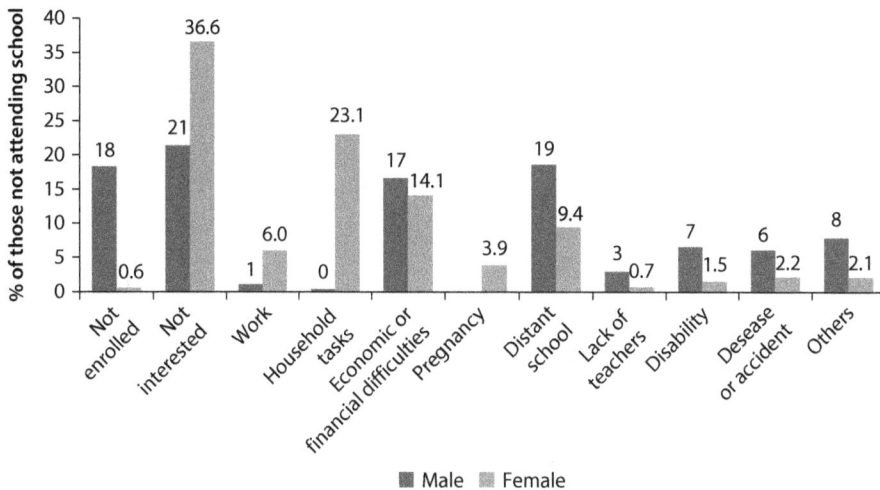

Source: World Bank calculations based on analysis of household surveys.

Toward More Efficient and Effective Public Social Spending in Central America
http://dx.doi.org/10.1596/978-1-4648-1060-2

Almeida, Fitszimons, and Rogers (forthcoming) stress the importance for LAC and Central America, in particular, of conducting better assessments and piloting evaluating policies so that interventions are supported by empirical evidence. In addition, they argue that some of the highest-return demand-side policies are likely deferred scholarships, conditional cash transfers (CCTs), and providing information about returns to education, although there is large diversity in their cost-effectiveness. Further, extending the number of compulsory years of full-time schooling, school-based management, reduced teen pregnancy, and socio-emotional training with supplemental academic tutoring are also promising.

Tertiary enrollment and graduation rates in the Central America subregion are generally low (2,984 per 100,000 inhabitants) and increasing very slowly in most countries; there is somewhat more rapid progress in enrollment and graduation only in Costa Rica and Nicaragua. Average years of tertiary education are lower than expected in Costa Rica, where they are well below levels in countries with similar gross domestic product (GDP) per capita such as Chile and Mexico. Average years of tertiary education are higher than expected in Nicaragua and Panama, given GDP per capita (figure 4.19). The low primary and secondary graduation rates in Nicaragua may indicate too large a focus on tertiary education. In part, slow progress in tertiary enrollment (figure 4.20) is the result of low quality and high dropout rates in upper secondary education.

Figure 4.19 Average Years of Tertiary Schooling, Ages 25–29, Compared with GDP per Capita, 2012

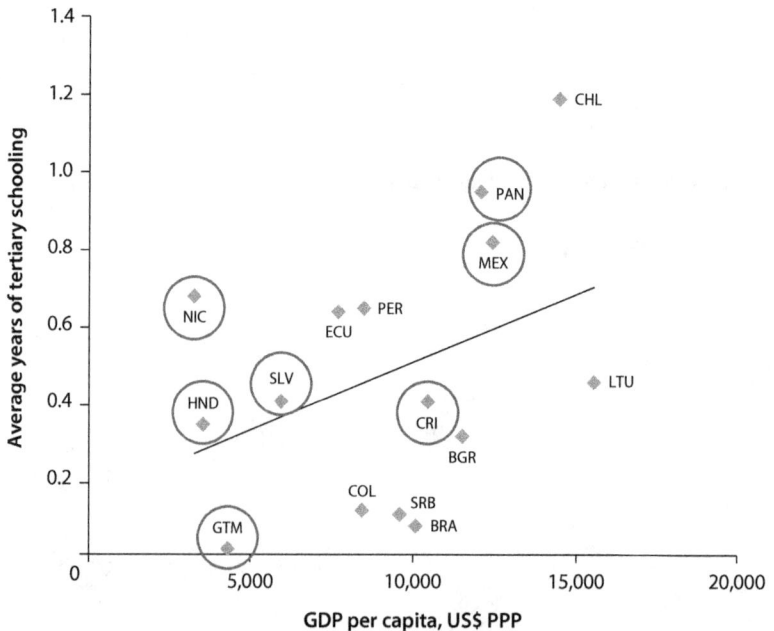

Source: Edstats, World Bank.
Note: BGR = Bulgaria; BRA = Brazil; CHL = Chile; COL = Colombia; CRI = Costa Rica; ECU = Ecuador; GTM = Guatemala; HND = Honduras; LTU = Lithuania; MEX = Mexico; NIC = Nicaragua; PAN = Panama; PER = Peru; SLV = El Salvador; SRB = Serbia; PPP = purchasing power parity.

As with secondary completion, students from higher-income households are more likely to enroll and graduate from colleges and universities. Students in tertiary education are disproportionately from wealthier households (42 percent of students enrolled in tertiary education in Panama are in the top income quintile), and public spending on tertiary education disproportionately goes to higher-income households (figure 4.21). This is the opposite of primary education, where students are disproportionately from low-income households, and public spending disproportionately benefits lower-income quintiles.

Figure 4.20 Enrollment in Tertiary Education per 100,000 Inhabitants, by Country

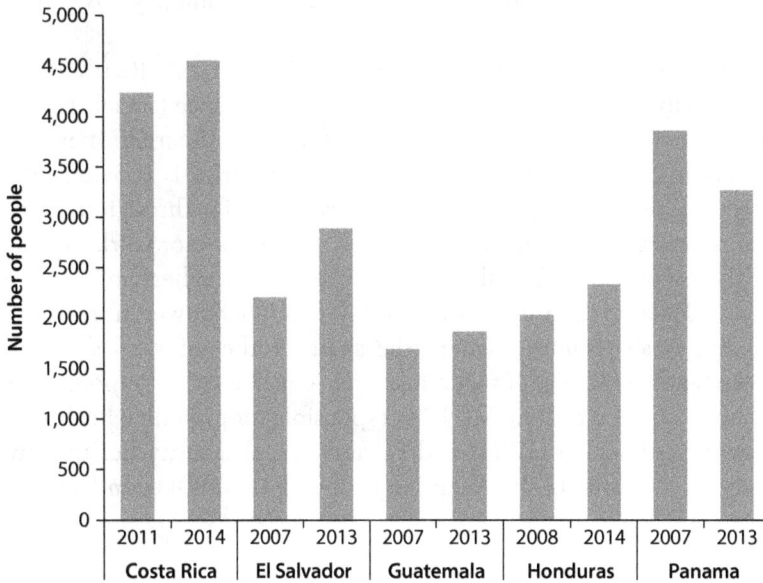

Sources: EdStats; UNESCO Institute for Statistics; World Bank.

Figure 4.21 Distribution of Total Students in Panama, by Level and Income Quintile, 2013

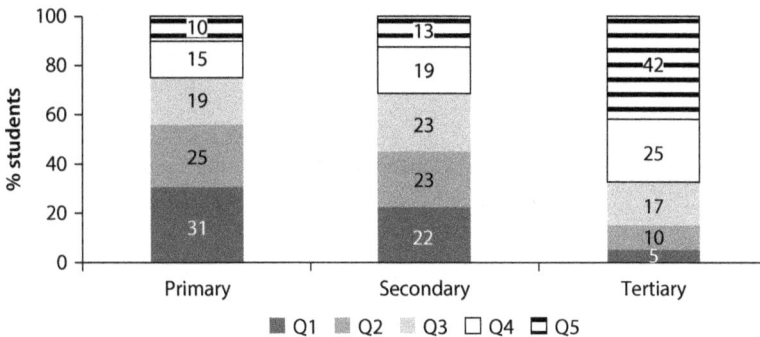

Sources: World Bank analysis of household surveys; calculations using standardized ADePT.

Toward More Efficient and Effective Public Social Spending in Central America
http://dx.doi.org/10.1596/978-1-4648-1060-2

Health Care Coverage and Targeting

With the exception of Costa Rica, where the Social Security Institute is the main health services provider, the Ministry of Health (MOH) provides the majority of health services in the rest of Central America (figure 4.22). Even in Panama, where social security covers 81.4 percent of the population, the MOH provides services to 33 percent of social security beneficiaries (combined with the noninsured, this implies that approximately 53 percent of health services in Panama are provided by the MOH). However, although the MOH is supposed to cover most of the population, especially the uninsured, service coverage gaps exist. For example, despite efforts to use mobile health teams and other alternative service delivery models, estimated service coverage gaps are greater than 30 percent in Guatemala and approximately 18 percent in Honduras.

Social security health insurance coverage is high in Costa Rica and Panama, while in El Salvador, Guatemala, and Honduras, insurance (social security and prepaid schemes) coverage is concentrated among the rich (figure 4.23). Public health insurance in Central American countries is provided through social security. Social security in all countries is paid for through payroll taxes and is thus hard to obtain for self-employed, informal sector workers and those out of the labor force. Social security coverage is highest in Costa Rica,[5] followed by Panama (figures 4.22 and 4.24). It is much lower in the rest of the Central American countries where the share of the informal sector in the workforce tends to be high. Private insurance coverage is even more limited in these other countries, but the MOH is responsible for providing health services to the uninsured. In Costa Rica and Panama, social security health insurance allows access to public health facilities, including the MOH-run facilities.

Figure 4.22 Coverage of Health Providers in Central America

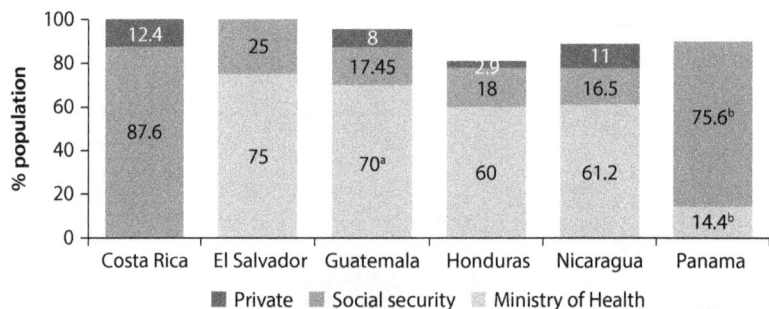

Source: PAHO 2012.

a. In Guatemala, recent estimates of MOH coverage have decreased to approximately 50 percent because the MOH discontinued the Programa de Extension de Cobertura (Extension of Coverage Program), and the MOH is still in the process of rolling out its new model of care.

b. A more recent estimate of social security coverage in Panama is 81 percent, and the MOH is estimated to provide a much higher percentage of services.

Figure 4.23 Insurance Coverage, by Quintile

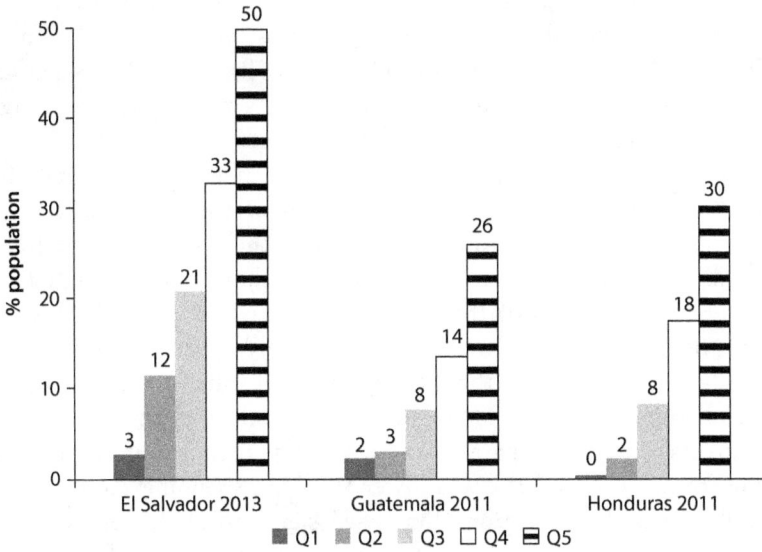

Sources: World Bank analysis of household surveys; calculations using standardized ADePT software
(Health Module).

Figure 4.24 Insurance Coverage, by Country

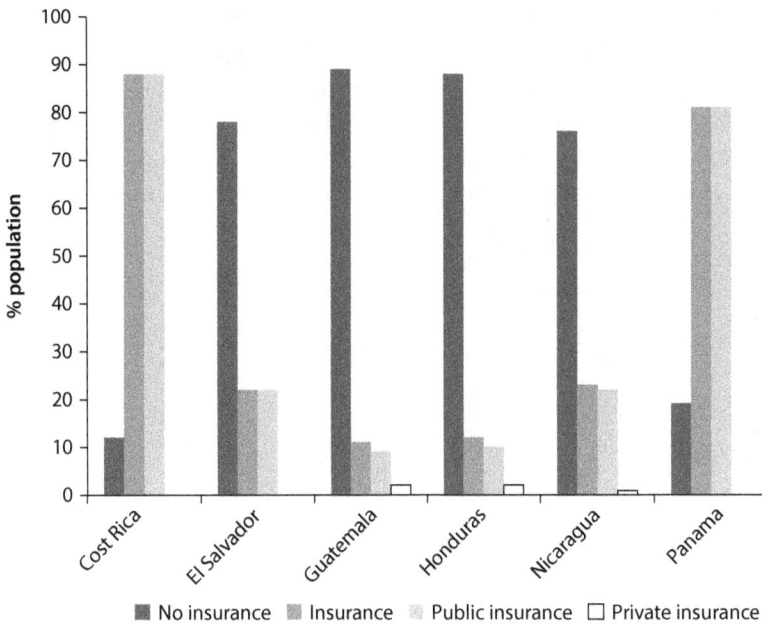

Sources: World Bank analysis of household surveys; staff calculations using standardized ADePT software
(Health Module).

Even in countries where the MOH covers the majority of the population, per capita spending by social security is still higher than per capita spending by the MOH. Although the MOH covers most of the population in El Salvador, Honduras, Guatemala, and Nicaragua (figure 4.22), its per capita spending tends to be lower than social security's per capita spending. For example, in Guatemala, MOH spending per capita was 22 percent of social security's per capita spending, despite the fact that the Guatemala Social Security Institute covers only about one-fifth of the population that the MOH covers. In Honduras, from 2007 to 2010, the Social Security Institute spent significantly more than the MOH, even though its estimated coverage was less than a third of the MOH's estimated coverage. In Nicaragua, although the Social Security Institute covers only approximately a third of the population covered by the MOH, its per capita spending is at least 11 percent higher than MOH spending. In El Salvador, the MOH has the largest coverage rate in Central America (75 percent), but its increase in spending from 2007 to 2012 was lower than the spending increase of four other public health institutions that have significantly lower coverage. In 2012, for example, per capita expenditures were US$114 by the MOH, US$237 by the Social Security Institute, US$251 by the Military Health Unit (Comando de Sanidad Militar, COSAM), and US$528 by the teachers' institute (Instituto Salvadoreno de Bienestar Magisterial, ISBM).

Overall, service coverage rates have increased, but access to health services is higher in urban areas, for the highest income quintile, and for the nonindigenous. Costa Rica, for example, has achieved almost universal access to basic care, and utilization of health care is high across all income quintiles (figure 4.25).[6] Overall health service coverage rates in the rest of the Central American countries have also increased since 2007. However, in a number of Central American countries, significant gaps remain in access to quality health care between urban areas and rural areas, across income quintiles, and between

Figure 4.25 Outpatient Visits in Costa Rica, by Income Quintile, 2006

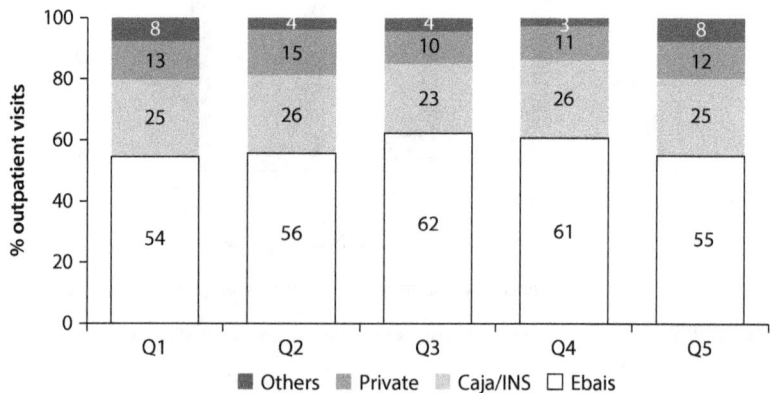

Source: ENSA 2006.

nonindigenous and indigenous populations. For example, in Guatemala, access to prenatal care provided by a medical doctor is almost three times higher for women in the highest-income quintile than for those in the lowest quintile, and almost two times higher for nonindigenous women than for indigenous women (figure 4.26). Similarly, in Honduras, access to a doctor for prenatal care is lowest for indigenous women and lower for rural women than for women in urban areas (figure 4.27).

In several countries, a high percentage of the sick did not consult a health care provider, especially among the poor. A large share of the people who reported an illness during the surveys conducted in Guatemala, Honduras, El Salvador, and Nicaragua did not seek medical care. An even larger proportion of the people in the lowest income quintile did not seek care compared to the people in the highest income quintile (figure 4.28). The main reasons cited by the poor for not seeking care are that their illness was not serious and they did not have sufficient funds (figure 4.29). Of those who did seek care, a significantly higher proportion of the people in the lowest income quintile went to public providers compared to those in the highest income quintile, who tended to go to private providers (figure 4.28).

El Salvador, Guatemala, and Nicaragua have eliminated user fees in MOH facilities to address the issue of lack of funds, which is commonly cited by the poor as a major constraint to seeking care. The Government of Guatemala

Figure 4.26 Prenatal Care Provided by Medical Doctor, Guatemala, 2014/15

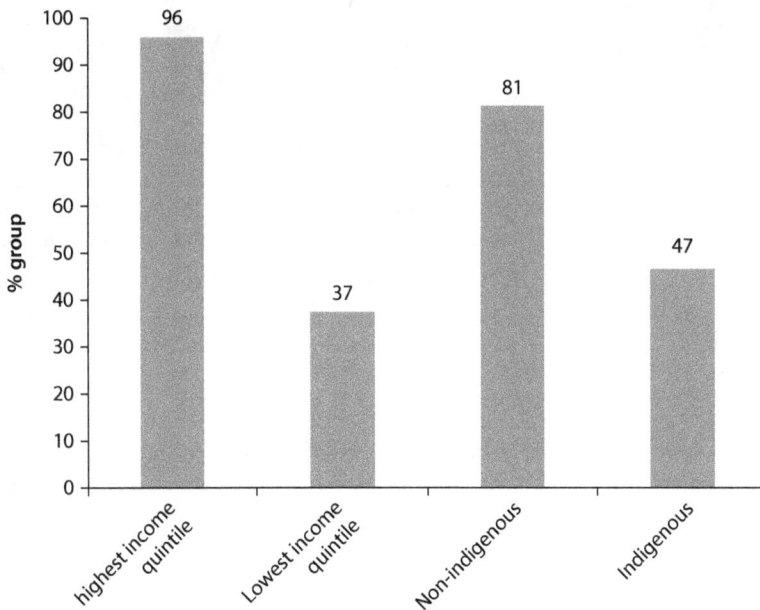

Source: Guatemala National Maternal and Child Health and Nutrition Survey 2014/15.

Toward More Efficient and Effective Public Social Spending in Central America
http://dx.doi.org/10.1596/978-1-4648-1060-2

Figure 4.27 Prenatal Care Provided by Medical Doctor, Honduras, 2011

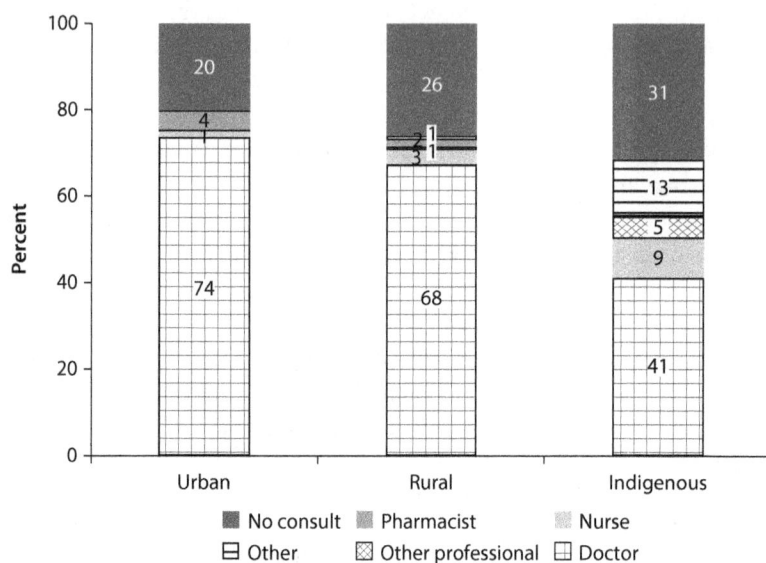

Source: Honduras Demographic and Health Survey.

Figure 4.28 Share of the Sick Who Did Not Consult a Provider, and Who Consulted Public or Private Health Providers, by Country and Income Quintile

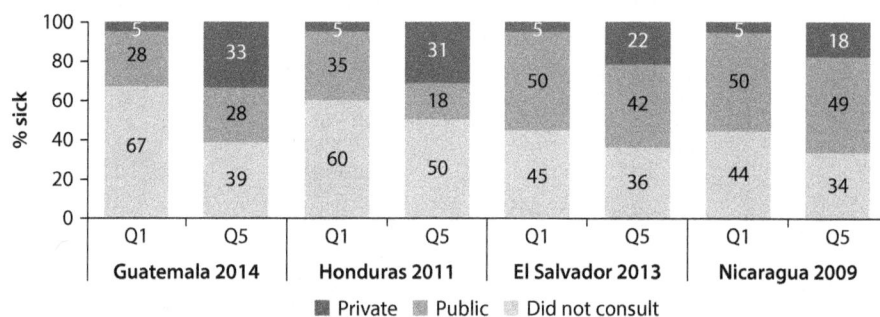

Sources: World Bank analysis of household surveys; calculations using standardized ADePT software (Health Module).

eliminated user fees in MOH facilities in 2008. However, out-of-pocket shares of total health spending have only decreased from 56 percent in 2008 to 52 percent in 2014 (World Bank 2015), and patients have been reported to seek care in the private sector and pay for medicines, because several public health facilities do not have the required inputs. The elimination of fee-for-service has, however, had a positive impact on health care use in El Salvador and Nicaragua.

Figure 4.29 Main Reasons for Not Consulting, by Income Quintile

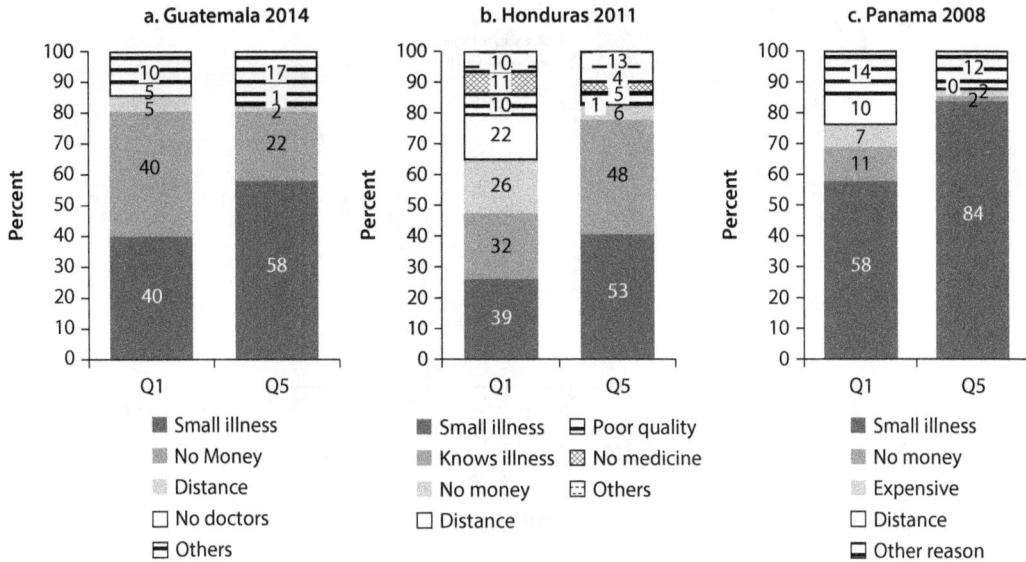

a. Guatemala 2014   b. Honduras 2011   c. Panama 2008

Sources: World Bank analysis of household surveys; calculations using standardized ADePT software (Health Module).

In particular, in 2009, El Salvador's MOH eliminated user fees in all its facilities and created the Network of Integrated Health Care Services (RIIS), expanding and promoting the integration of health coverage to the population. As a result of these combined changes, from 2008 to 2012, households in the lower two expenditure quintiles that sought care at public health facilities increased by approximately 8 percentage points, while households in the highest expenditure quintile that sought care at public health care facilities increased by more than 10 percentage points (figure 4.30). In Nicaragua, the number of primary health care (PHC) consultations increased from 8.5 million in 2006 to 16.7 million visits in 2013, and hospital-based consultations rose from 1.3 million in 2006 to 3.1 million in 2013.

To address service coverage gaps and improve the utilization of services, Costa Rica, El Salvador, Guatemala, Honduras, and Panama use mobile teams to provide health care to rural and isolated communities. In Costa Rica, El Salvador, Guatemala, and Panama mobile teams are government staffed, although Guatemala used to contract nongovernmental organizations that deployed mobile teams under the Programa de Extensión de Cobertura (Extension of Coverage Program) until early 2015 (box 4.1 provides more details on efforts by other countries to improve coverage). Honduras has a decentralized model of care in a number of areas where community-based organizations, foundations, or groups of munici-palities (*mancomunidades*) operate facilities in areas where there is no MOH facility. They receive MOH funding based on performance.

Figure 4.30 Health Care Visits, by Level of Care, El Salvador, 2008–12

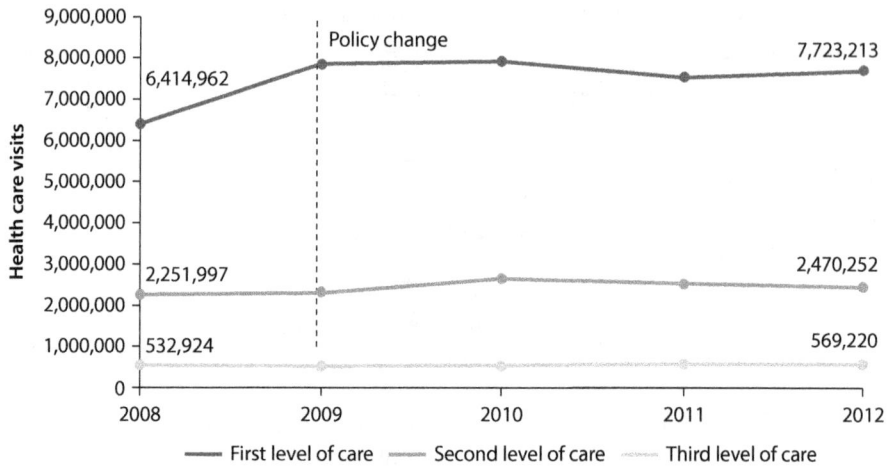

Source: Ministry of Health, El Salvador.

Box 4.1 Expanding Health Coverage in Costa Rica, El Salvador, and Panama through Mobile Teams

Near-universal access to primary health care (PHC) in **Costa Rica** is the responsibility of the Equipo Básico de Atención Integral de Salud (Basic Team for Integrated Health Care; EBAIS), with 1,013 staff and 817 clinics. EBAIS health care clinics cover 94 percent of the population and are located throughout the country, even in the most inaccessible rural and indigenous areas. The most remote clinics, *puestos de visita periódica*, are staffed only periodically by EBAIS personnel. An EBAIS is an integrated team that includes at a minimum one primary care physician, a nurse, a technical assistant with specialization in primary care, a medical registry technician, and a pharmacist. In some cases, the team also includes a nutritionist and psychologist. The EBAIS health care clinics provide primary care to all people in an area. In addition to clinic visits, a technical assistant who specializes in primary care visits each home in the EBAIS region and identifies possible health risks. If health risks are found, the technical assistant will arrange for a visit to the physician and act as case manager when PHC is being provided. This activity has been particularly important in bringing PHC to families in isolated rural and indigenous communities.

In **El Salvador**, the government is expanding coverage of health services through implementation of Equipos Comunitarios de Salud (Family Community Teams; ECOS). ECOS are health teams that visit the rural areas to provide health care at the household level with both general and specialized care. This service is considered innovative because it harmonized the way PHC was delivered, especially in poor rural areas. Previously, these health services were provided by nongovernmental organizations, which were more costly and less harmonized, especially with the rest of the health system. By 2013, 517 ECOS have been deployed in

box continues next page

Box 4.1 Expanding Health Coverage in Costa Rica, El Salvador, and Panama through Mobile Teams *(continued)*

62 percent (164) of the country's municipalities. The ECOS mobile health teams have increased service coverage and helped solve overcrowding in hospitals in some regions. However, the sustainability of this model is at stake because it has not been considered in budget planning and budget projections, and it is partially funded by international partners. In addition, the ECOS mobile health teams are relatively larger (8–12 people) than the usual two to four health professionals of other traditional mobile community teams.

In 2003, to address the issue of inequitable health access for the poor, **Panama**'s MOH implemented an expanded national program, Estrategia de Extensión de Cobertura (Strategy for Coverage Extension; EEC). This program aimed to extend coverage of, and increase access to, PHC services. The program included the delivery of the Paquete Integral de Servicios de Salud (Integrated Package of Health Care Services; PAISS) to remote, rural, and indigenous areas, using capitation payments that created financial incentives for providers to achieve better results—a results-based financing approach. After five years of the PAISS experience, the MOH took the EEC to the next level by launching the Health Protection for Vulnerable Populations Program in 2008, providing health services to the rural poor by way of mobile health teams. This program also uses a results-based financing approach, financing results-adjusted capitation payments to the health regions to promote improvements in coverage and performance.

Social Protection and Labor Coverage and Targeting

Social protection spending in Central America is dominated by contributory pensions, which have limited coverage and are overall regressive. There are two types of public pensions in Central America: contributory and noncontributory (social pensions). Coverage of contributory pensions is limited by the degree of formalization in the labor market in general. With the exception of Costa Rica and Panama (where 69 percent and 60 percent of workers, respectively, contribute to social security), coverage is well below the Latin American average, accounting for less than 20 percent of workers in Guatemala and Honduras (figure 4.31). Coverage of contributory pensions among the elderly is also low and, not surprisingly, concentrated among wealthier households (figure 4.32). Consequently, as happens all across Latin America, contributory pension payments are overall regressive, even though the majority of pay-as-you-go schemes that predominate in Central America[7] are heavily subsidized to provide minimum legislated benefits.

Low coverage of contributory pensions spurred the creation of several noncontributory (or social) schemes, which are in general well targeted in Costa Rica, El Salvador, Nicaragua, and Panama, but not in Honduras and Guatemala. Social pensions have emerged to fill a coverage gap in Costa Rica, Panama, and Nicaragua, reaching between 15 percent and 25 percent of the elderly. In those

Figure 4.31 Share of Workers Contributing to Social Security, by Country, circa 2014

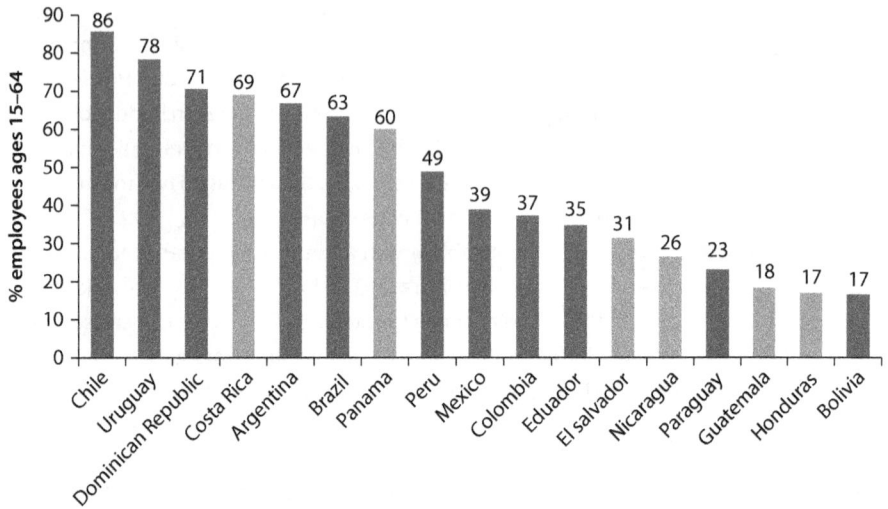

Source: World Bank LAC Equity Lab.

Figure 4.32 Share of Elderly Covered by Pensions, by Income Quintile

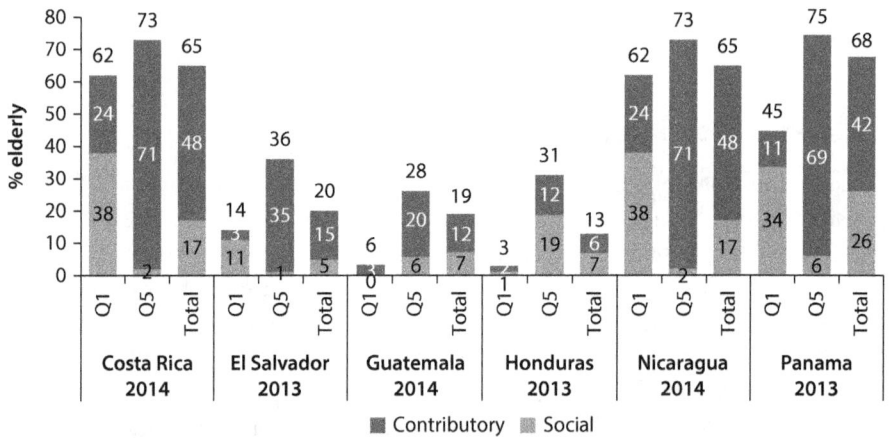

Source: World Bank analysis of household surveys; calculations using standardized ADePT software (Social Protection Module).

countries, social pension coverage among the poorest 20 percent oscillates between 35 percent and 40 percent, with leakages to the nonpoor at minimum levels, revealing overall good targeting. In contrast, social pension coverage is below 10 percent in El Salvador, Guatemala, and Honduras, and in general is not well targeted in Guatemala, and Honduras, with only 1 percent of households in the lowest income quintile receiving social pensions (while among households in the top income quintile, 19 percent in Honduras and 6 percent in Guatemala receive these noncontributory pensions). In many of these countries, migrant remittances are helping cover expenses for the elderly (in Honduras, 16 percent of the elderly, and in Nicaragua 31 percent, receive remittances but no pension, according to Bebczuk and Battistón 2010).

Considering both contributory and noncontributory pensions, the overall picture is of high regressivity in the majority of countries in Central America. Despite advances in filling coverage gaps with social pensions, half of the beneficiaries of pensions in El Salvador belong to the top income quintile, reaching close to 60 percent in Guatemala and Honduras (figure 4.33). In Costa Rica and Panama, which are the Central American countries with the most comprehensive social pension schemes, the distribution is much more equal (at least with regard to access; benefits are still unequal even in these countries).

CCT programs are generally narrowly targeted toward the poor, but coverage is lowest in countries with programs that have more progressive incidence. CCT programs have been at the forefront of the targeting revolution. Introduced in 64 countries, today five out of six of the Central American countries studied in this report have a CCT program. CCTs generally provide cash transfers to families conditional on children remaining in school and/or regularly visiting health clinics and/or some sort of job training for parents. Many CCTs show quite good poor-targeting performance, with Guatemala, Honduras, and Panama standing out as the most accurate in reaching the poor (more than 85 percent of beneficiaries below the national poverty line). In other countries, such as Costa Rica, targeting accuracy is less impressive, which is a reflection of a weak or outdated information system. In others, such as El Salvador, errors of exclusion are substantial since the program size is so small that a large proportion of the poor are left out (for example, it operates in only 100 of 262 municipalities). In most countries, even with good targeting, reaching the poorest (the bottom 20 percent of

Figure 4.33 Distribution of Pension Beneficiaries among the Elderly, by Income Quintile and Country

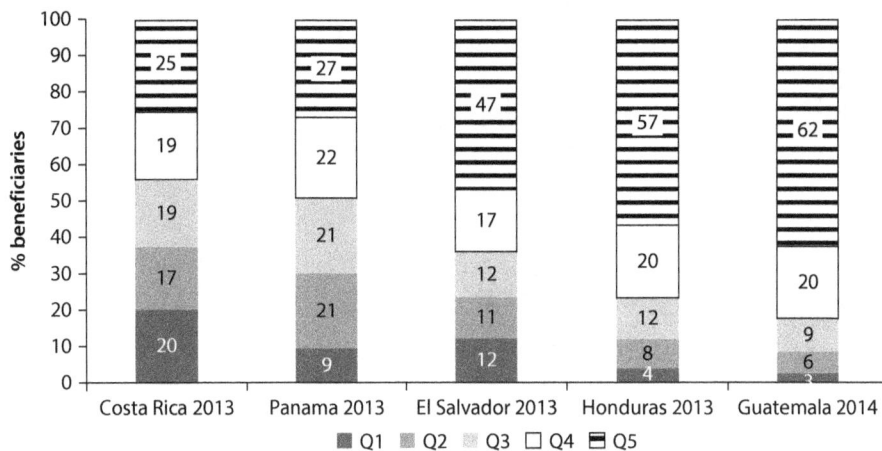

Sources: World Bank analysis of household surveys; calculations using standardized ADePT software (Social Protection Module).

Toward More Efficient and Effective Public Social Spending in Central America
http://dx.doi.org/10.1596/978-1-4648-1060-2

the income distribution) has been difficult. Only Panama, where 72 percent of beneficiaries belong to the poorest 20 percent, stands out among Central American countries (figure 4.34).[8] Another contribution of CCTs is that they are often introduced along with a major data collection exercise to identify poor beneficiaries through proxy means or means-tested formulas. These data are often subsequently used by other programs to share a common targeting approach and, in the best of cases, are the initial step toward building social beneficiary registries.

Overall, equalizing the distributional effectiveness of social assistance programs should improve; many of the benefits of these interventions are paid to the nonpoor. While in general, CCTs and social pensions are well targeted, this is not the case with many other social assistance interventions that represent a large proportion of resources (figure 4.35). In most countries much of social assistance spending is for universally available programs that are not well targeted (for example, school feeding and consumption subsidies). Extreme cases where such subsidies are regressive include electricity subsidies in Honduras (more than 40 percent of beneficiaries belong to the top two quintiles of the distribution), in-kind food for the elderly in Costa Rica (37 percent to the richest 40 percent), and scholarships in Panama (25 percent to the top 40 percent). There is substantial room for improvement in focusing social assistance to the most needy.

Little is known about the distributional incidence of ALMPs, but the scant evidence suggests there is considerable room to improve access for priority groups such as the unemployed and the poor. Few of the programs report beneficiaries by socioeconomic status or categorical groups. One of the exceptions is the Instituto Nacional Tecnológico (National Institute of Technology, INATEC) in Nicaragua, the national training institution in the Central American region with the highest budget as a share of the GDP (0.5 percent compared to an

Figure 4.34 Public Spending and Share of Beneficiaries of Main CCTs, by Country

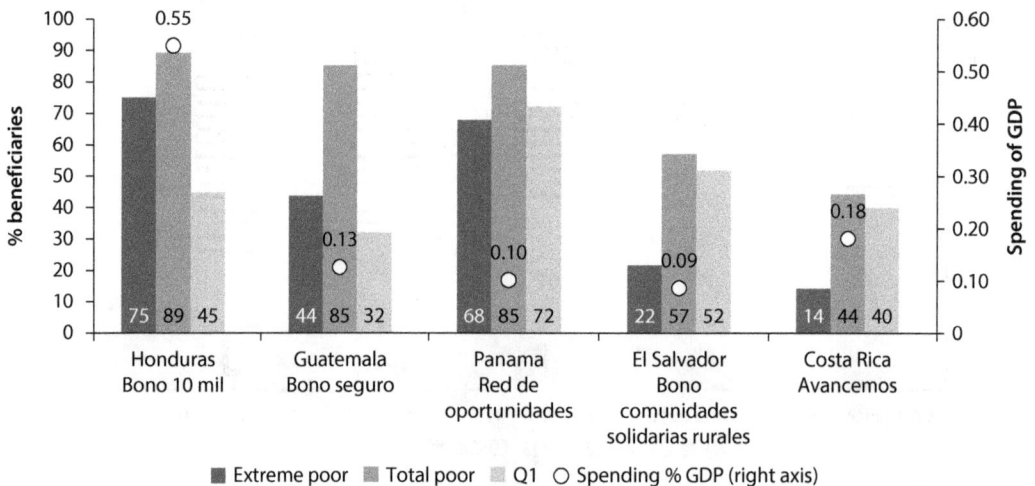

Extreme poor ■ Total poor ■ Q1 ■ Spending % GDP (right axis) ○

Sources: World Bank analysis of household surveys; calculations using standardized ADePT software (Social Protection Module).

Figure 4.35 Distribution of Social Assistance Program Benefits

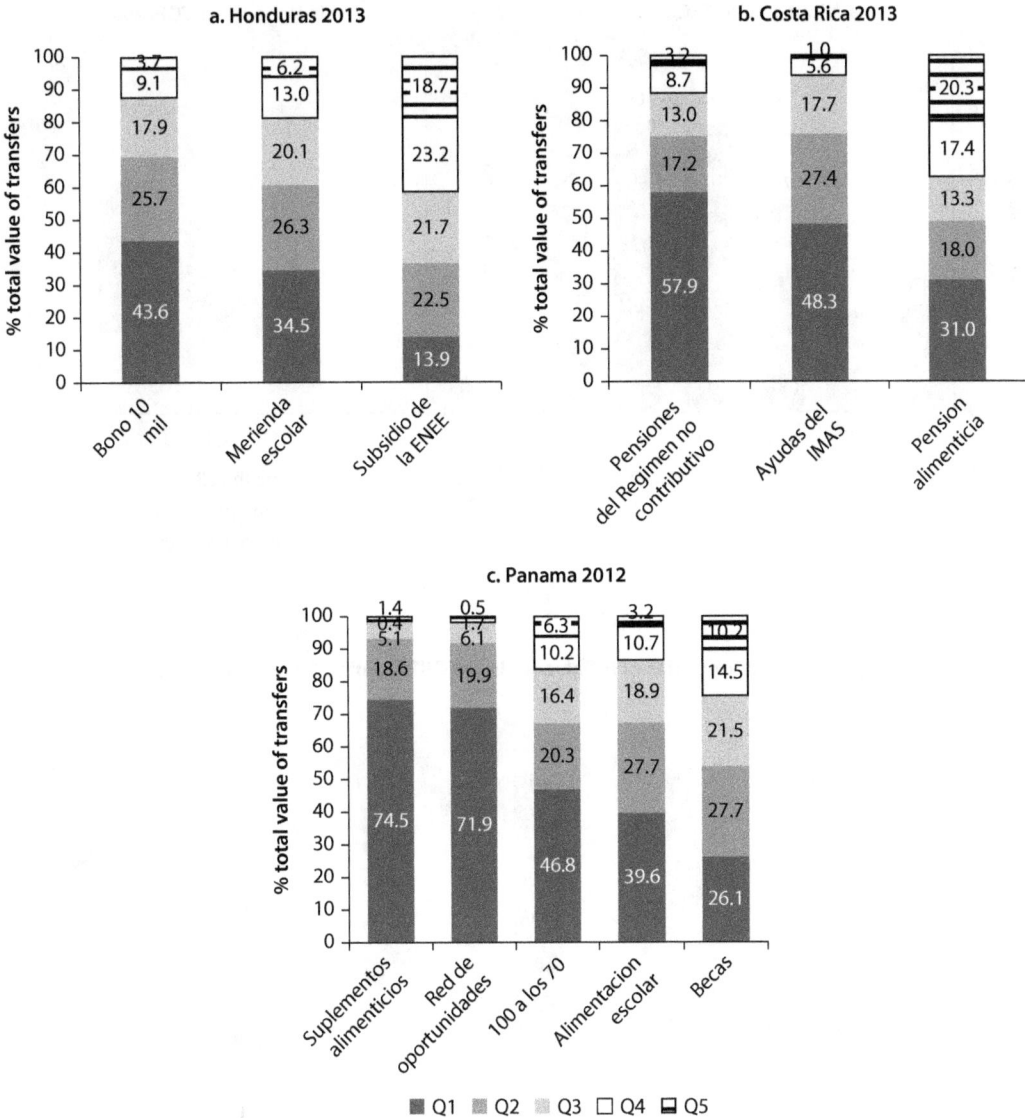

a. Honduras 2013

b. Costa Rica 2013

c. Panama 2012

■ Q1 ▦ Q2 ▨ Q3 □ Q4 ▱ Q5

Sources: World Bank analysis of household surveys; calculations using standardized ADePT software (Social Protection Module).

average of 0.2 in the other countries). From 2007 to 2013, its coverage tripled from 73,807 to 315,729 trainees.

However, several disparities are found by income quintile. Just 4 percent of participants in training courses belonged to the bottom 40 percent of the distribution, compared to 10 percent among the top 40 percent (figure 4.36). Similar figures were found for Honduras in an earlier analysis of coverage of the Instituto Nacional de Formación Profesional (National Institute for Professional Training; INFOP) of unemployed participants by income quintile (figure 4.36). This is not

Figure 4.36 Coverage of Unemployed, by Income Quintile

a. Nicaragua INATEC, 2014

b. Honduras INFOP, 2007

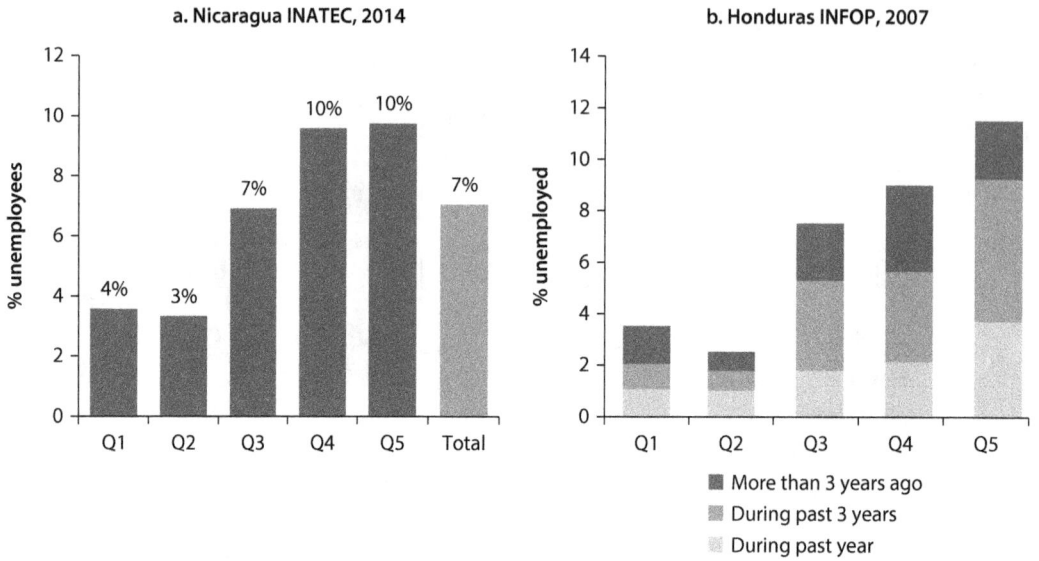

■ More than 3 years ago
▨ During past 3 years
░ During past year

Source: World Bank analysis of household surveys.

Figure 4.37 Beneficiaries of El Salvador INSAFORP Training Courses, 2009–13

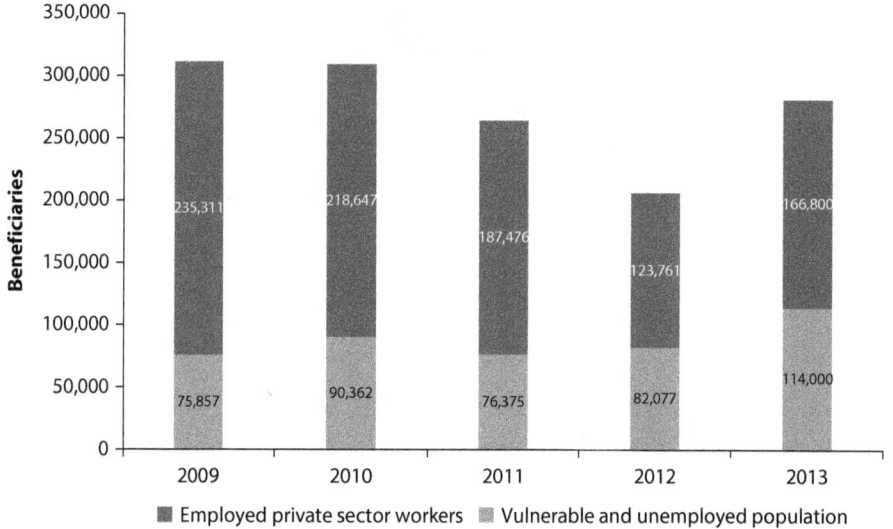

■ Employed private sector workers   ▨ Vulnerable and unemployed population

Sources: World Bank analysis of household surveys; calculations using standardized ADePT software (Labor ILO Module).

surprising since many technical training courses require a minimum qualification level, typically high school graduation. In general, most of the beneficiaries of training courses are employed private sector workers, as opposed to being unemployed (as administrative records from El Salvador's Institute for Professional Training, INSAFORP, show; see figure 4.37).

Figure 4.38 Distribution of Guatemala INTECAP Beneficiaries, by Age, 2011

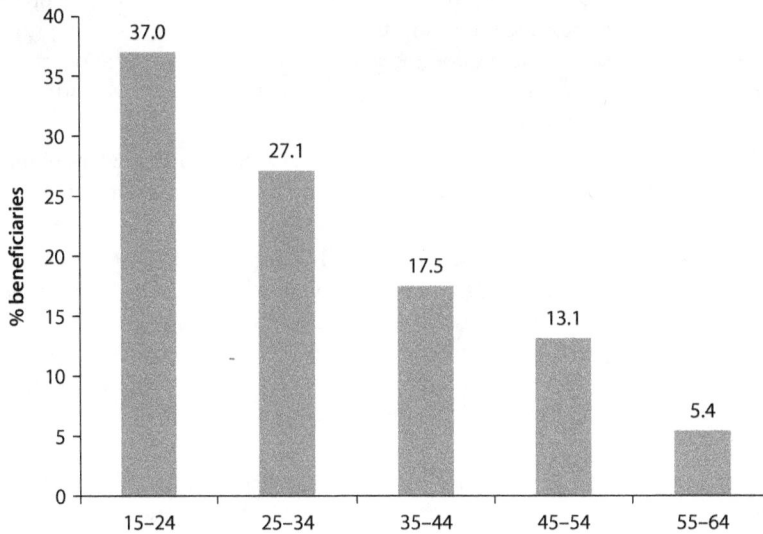

Source: INSAFORP.

There is also a big generational divide in access, with youth typically benefiting the most from these training opportunities. Recent evidence from the program of Guatemala's national training institution, the Instituto Técnico de Capacitación y Productividad (Technical Training and Productivity Institute; INTECAP) found that two-thirds of participants were under 34 years old (figure 4.38). This leads to doubts about the real opportunities these programs provide for adults to reskill when they lose their jobs.

Notes

1. Net primary school enrollment rates in Guatemala fell from 2008 to 2014. One possible reason for this is that the latest available population estimates are based on predictions from the 2002 census. If the population grew less than predicted, there may be fewer children missing from school than the numbers suggest. It may also be that the net enrollment rate in 2008 and 2009 was unusually high. The unusually high net enrollment rates in Guatemala in these years were likely due to the initiation of the CCT Mi Familia Progresa (My Family Progresses, MIFAPRO). Because MIFAPRO rewarded families for sending children to preprimary and primary school, there was a temporary increase in enrollments as children who had been kept out of school now enrolled for their families to obtain the CCT (Asociación Civil Educación para Todos and UNICEF 2016).

2. The model includes several dimensions to promote quality, including (a) development, design, and implementation of new curriculum and learning instruments for preschool; (b) promotion of, and incentivizing teacher participation in, preservice

training to obtain a teacher certificate; (c) development and piloting of new quality standards for preschool infrastructure; (d) delivery of learning materials to preschools nationwide (such as puzzles, musical instruments, and small supplies); and (e) establishment of an early childhood development monitoring and evaluation system. To date, over 20 percent of the nongraduated community teachers have participated in preservice training and now hold a teacher's certificate.

3. Lack of interest may also be related to demand-side factors such as a lack of information about returns to schooling and supply-side factors such as mismatch of curriculum and job market needs.

4. Migration of a family member might also lead to increased family income through remittances. The higher income may make good schools more affordable for the children left behind. However, some studies find that the negative effect of the migration of a parent outweighs the positive effect of remittances (Amuedo-Dorantes and Pozo 2010). The negative impact on schooling is larger if mothers migrate than if fathers migrate, and the impact is larger on girls than on boys (Acosta 2011a, 2011b for El Salvador).

5. Costa Rica's almost universal insurance coverage has been achieved through the expansion of a single social insurance scheme, partly a consequence of a successful integration of the Social Security Institute (for the formally employed) and MOH, whereby the former absorbed the facilities of the latter during the 1990s. As part of this integration, a publicity and enforcement campaign was directed at self-employed and informal sector workers. Health insurance for the self-employed is subsidized—50 percent of social security health insurance payments for the self-employed are paid by the central government. In Costa Rica, a much smaller proportion of the workforce is in the informal sector than in other Central American countries (WHO website; Costa Rica Case Study).

6. Costa Rica has a long primary care tradition, and the Caja Costaricense de Seguridad Social (Costa Rican Social Security Fund; CCSS) manages an extensive network of primary and basic specialized services. Despite the rise in private spending, utilization rates of public facilities remain high, and public institutions provide over 80 percent of services. Utilization of public outpatient services is similar for all quintiles, and surveyed individuals from all income groups consider the CCSS as the most important ambulatory provider for ambulatory health services (PHC or Equipo Básico de Atencion Integral de Salud [Basic Team for Integrated Health Attention; EBAIS] and specialized care provided by the CCSS).

7. With the exception of El Salvador, which reformed its system to use individual savings accounts.

8. However, this may be because Panama's CCT program is smaller in coverage and spending than other CCTs in the subregion (it has not been subject to rapid and massive scale-up that usually undermines targeting accuracy).

References

Acosta, P. 2011a. "School Attendance, Child Labor, and Remittances from International Migration in El Salvador." *Journal of Development Studies* 47 (6): 913–36.

———. 2011b. "Female Migration and Child Occupation in Rural El Salvador." *Population Research and Policy Review* 30 (4): 569–89.

Adelman, M. A., and M. Szekely. 2016. "School Dropout in Central America: An Overview of Trends, Causes, Consequences, and Promising Interventions." Policy Research Working Paper 7561, World Bank, Washington, DC.

Almeida, R., E. Fitzsimons, and H. Rogers. Forthcoming. "How to Prevent Secondary-School Dropout in Latin America: Evidence from Rigorous Evaluations." Unpublished mimeo.

Amuedo-Dorantes, C., and S. Pozo. 2010. "Accounting for Remittance and Migration Effects on Children's Schooling." *World Development* 38 (12): 1747–59.

Asociación Civil Educación para Todos and UNICEF (United Nations International Children's Emergency Fund). 2016. *Los desafíos del cálculo de la cobertura en el sistema educativo.* Asociación Civil Educación para Todos; UNICEF.

Bebczuk, R., and D. Battistón. 2010. "Remittances and Life Cycle Deficits in Latin America." CEDLAS Working Paper 0094, CEDLAS, Universidad Nacional de La Plata, La Plata, Argentina.

Berlinski, S., and N. Schady. 2015. *The Early Years: Child Well-being and the Role of Public Policy.* Washington, DC: Inter-American Development Bank.

Chetty, R. J. N. Friedman, and J. E. Rocko. 2014. "Measuring the Impacts of Teachers II: Teacher Value-Added and Student Outcomes in adulthood." *American Economic Review* 104 (9): 2633–79.

ERCA (Programa Estado de la Región). 2016. "Quinto Informe Estado de la Region: El dilema estrategico de la educación en Centroamérica." Statistical Appendix. http://www.estadonacion.or.cr/erca2016/.

Hall, M. A. Singer, G. De Jong, and D. Roempke Graefe. 2011. "The Geography of Immigrant Skills." Brookings Policy Program June. https://www.brookings.edu/wp-content/uploads/2016/06/06_immigrants_singer.pdf.

McKenzie, D., and H. Rapoport. 2006. "Can Migration Reduce Educational Attainment?" Policy Research Working Paper 3952, World Bank, Washington, DC.

PEN (Programa Estado de la Nación). 2016. "Mejorar la educación: dilema estratégico para el desarrollo de Centroamérica." Quinto informe Estado de la Nación, Quito.

World Bank. 2015. *World Development Indicators 2015.* Washington, DC: World Bank.

CHAPTER 5

Effectiveness and Efficiency of Public Social Services

Effectiveness and Efficiency of Education Services

Primary school grade repetition and out-of-age enrollment are high in Central America. In no country is the out-of-age enrollment rate below the Latin America and the Caribbean (LAC) mean, and only in Panama is it close to the LAC mean. Primary school out-of-age enrollment rates are lower for girls than for boys in all countries (figure 5.1).

Compared to the LAC average, standardized test scores are low in Guatemala, Honduras, Nicaragua, and Panama.[1] These countries represent four of the bottom six countries in all tests where Third Regional Comparative and Explanatory Study (TERCE) tests were administered (3rd and 6th grade mathematics and reading; see figures 5.2–5.4). The low scores in Panama are especially alarming given that the relatively high gross domestic product (GDP) per capita in that country would predict high education quality results, and suggest that Panama has not taken full advantage of rapid growth to improve educational outcomes. El Salvador regularly administers country-specific standardized tests but did not participate in the Second Regional Comparative and Explanatory Study (SERCE), TERCE, or Programme for International Student Assessment (PISA). El Salvador did participate in the 2007 Trends in Mathematics and Science Study (TIMSS) 4th grade mathematics scores. These scores are also disappointing because they are much lower in El Salvador than countries with similar levels of GDP per capita (figure 5.5). Of Central American countries, standardized test scores are highest in Costa Rica.

Standardized test scores increased in Guatemala, Nicaragua, and Panama between 2006 and 2013, but not in Costa Rica and El Salvador.[2] Progress is most dramatic in Guatemala (figures 5.2–5.4). Most likely, the improvements in learning at the primary level in Guatemala are partly driven by the increase in the total number of teachers (by almost 50 percent in primary and by more in preschool) and in other resources, as shown by the increase in per student spending. In addition, falling enrollment at the primary level after 2010 could be leading

Figure 5.1 Primary School Out-of-Age Enrollment Rates, 2014

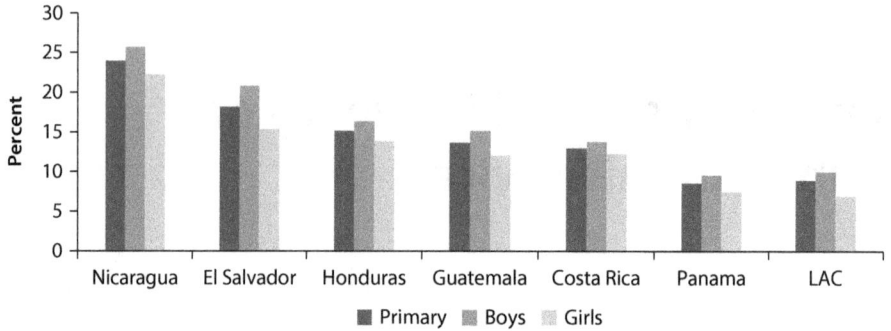

Sources: Bassi, Busso, and Munoz 2015; ERCA 2016.
Note: Overage rate = proportion of students who are enrolled in an education level who are outside the official age range
for that level. LAC figures are the average of 2006–10 given data availability of all countries.

Figure 5.2 Third-Grade Reading SERCE 2006 and TERCE 2013 Test Scores

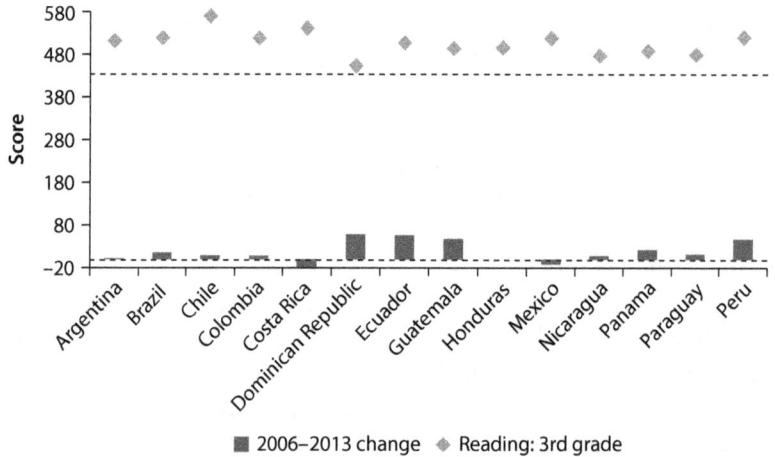

Sources: UNESCO 2015; Full TERCE Report.
Note: SERCE and TERCE were conducted by the Latin American Laboratory for Assessment of the Quality of
Education (LLECE) in 2006 and 2013. It tests reading, writing, and mathematics for students in 3rd and 6th
grades, with an additional natural sciences test for 6th graders. El Salvador is not a member of LLECE and
therefore did not participate on the tests. The average reflects the average of score and change levels for
all participating countries that took the reading exam.

to a composition effect in the sample, where the worst students leave school
before taking standardized tests.

While there was progress in Nicaragua, increases in standardized test scores
are lower in Nicaragua than in Guatemala. This may be because education policies in Nicaragua focused on a successful effort to improve access to and completion of primary school, and not on maintaining quality of resources and
teaching. SERCE/TERCE 6th grade mathematics scores fell in Costa Rica
between 2006 and 2013 (figure 5.4). The fall in 6th grade mathematics scores

Figure 5.3 Third-Grade Mathematics SERCE 2006 and TERCE 2013 Test Scores

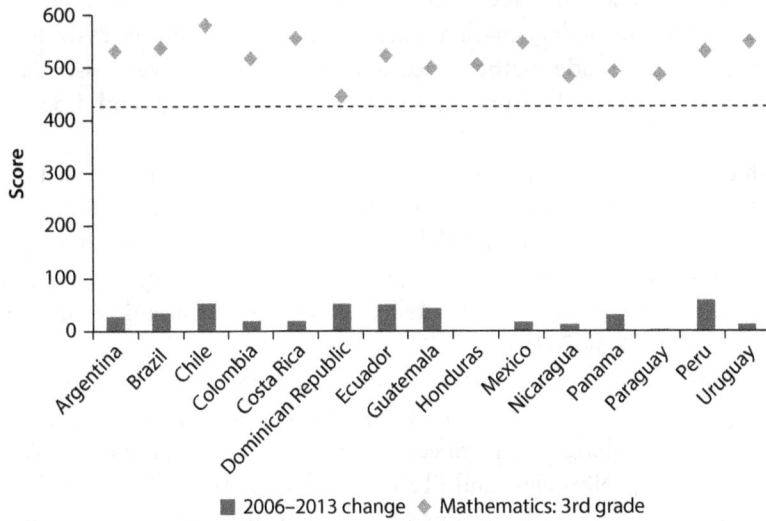

■ 2006–2013 change   ◆ Mathematics: 3rd grade

Source: UNESCO 2015, Full TERCE Report.
Note: The average reflects the average of score and change levels for all participating countries that took the reading exam.

Figure 5.4 SERCE/TERCE Comparative Results on Sixth-Grade Mathematics, 2006 and 2013

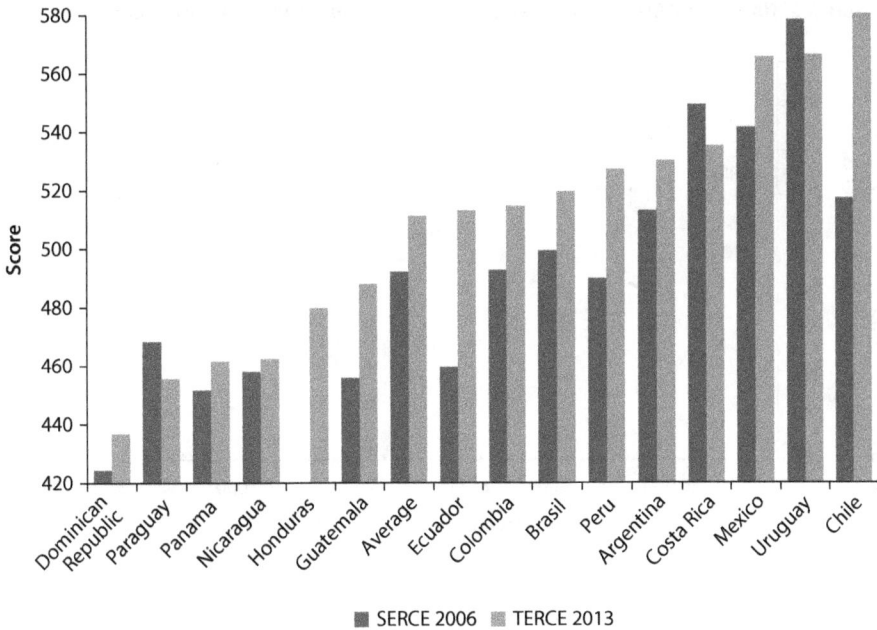

■ SERCE 2006   ▨ TERCE 2013

Source: UNESCO/LLECE.
Note: Honduras did not participate in SERCE in 2006.

Toward More Efficient and Effective Public Social Spending in Central America
http://dx.doi.org/10.1596/978-1-4648-1060-2

in Costa Rica is particularly disappointing given the significant increase in public spending on education in that country. National standardized tests in El Salvador show that upper secondary mathematics scores fell from 5.3 in 2007 to 4.2 in 2012, and that 3rd grade mathematics and language scores were essentially flat between 2005 and 2012—from 5.28 to 5.66 in mathematics and 5.55 to 5.72 in language.

Within countries, there is a positive correlation between income and student achievement (figure 5.6). Test scores are also lower for students in rural areas and those from lower-income families. This pattern is common throughout Central America and LAC. Even in Costa Rica, where learning outcomes at the primary level are relatively strong, large differences across socioeconomic groups persist (Adelman and Szekely 2016).

Rates of return to education (the value of education in the labor market) are falling in Nicaragua and El Salvador and rising in Costa Rica. Gindling and Trejos (2014) show that falling returns to education were the most important cause of falling inequality in Nicaragua and El Salvador from 2000 to 2009/10. There are several possible reasons why returns to education fell, including the declining quality of instruction, and the result of increased coverage that integrated less-skilled students into the educational system.[3]

Recent evidence clearly shows that simply more public spending on education is not sufficient to improve educational outcomes. In El Salvador, for example, increases in public spending on education were associated with better

Figure 5.5 TIMSS 2007 Mathematics, Fourth Grade, Compared with GDP per Capita

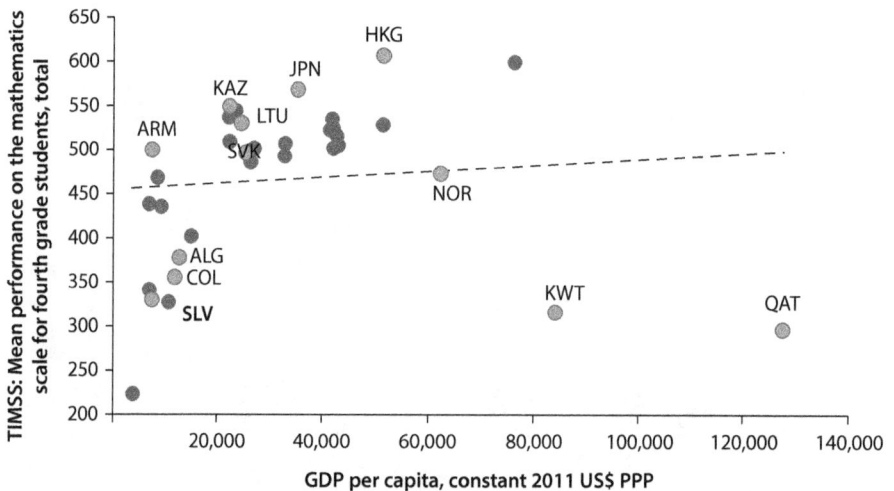

Source: Mullis, Martin, and Foy 2008.
Note: ALG = Algeria; ARM = Armenia; COL = Colombia; HKG = Hong Kong, China; JPN = Japan; KAZ = Kazakhstan; KWT = Kuwait; QAT = Qatar; LTU = Lithuania; NOR = Norway; PPP = purchasing power parity; SVK = Slovakia.

Figure 5.6 Relationship between Reading and TERCE Test Scores and Income

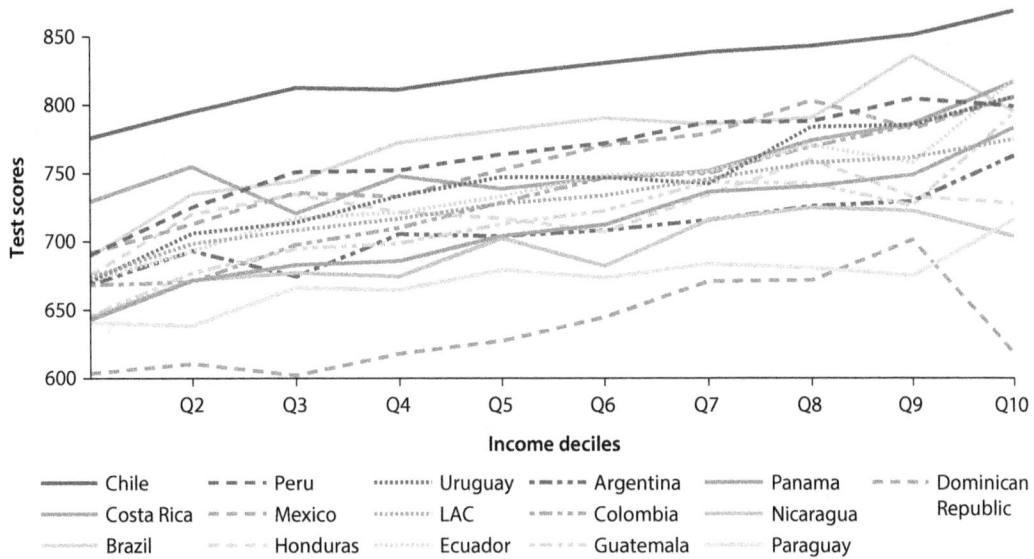

Source: Almeida and Oosterbeek 2016.

educational inputs, higher enrollment, and better access to schooling, but not with improvements in learning. Despite improvements in the "quantity" of educational inputs, as proxied by the student-teacher ratio, learning outcomes have not improved. Between 2007 and 2012, public spending on education per student in primary education increased on average by 42 percent, from US$547 to US$779 (figure 5.7). Nevertheless, a comparison of test score results in language and mathematics for 3rd graders, as measured by the country's own national test score (Prueba de Aprendizajes y Aptitudes para Egresados de Educación Básica, National Assessment of Learning Competencies for Basic Education Graduates; PAESITA), shows no change between 2005 and 2012 (figure 5.8). Moreover, while the average expenditure per student in upper secondary rose from US$802 in 2007 to US$811 in 2012, the average result in mathematics (as measured by the Prueba de Aprendizajes y Aptitudes para Egresados de Educación Media, National Assessment of Learning Competencies for Secondary School Graduates; PAES) dropped from 5.3 to 4.2 (figure 5.9).[4]

Furthermore, improvements in the "quality" of selected educational inputs, including of teachers and classroom teaching, coupled with strengthened accountability of teachers and directors, seems to be a necessary condition to improve learning outcomes (Bruns and Luque 2014). Low quality of teacher instruction, generated both by the low quality of teacher preparation and reduced teacher incentives to perform adequately, could partly explain poor results in test scores in Central America. Higher wages for teachers are not sufficient to improve learning. Teacher wages are high in the subregion compared

Figure 5.7 Public Spending in Education per Student in Primary School, El Salvador

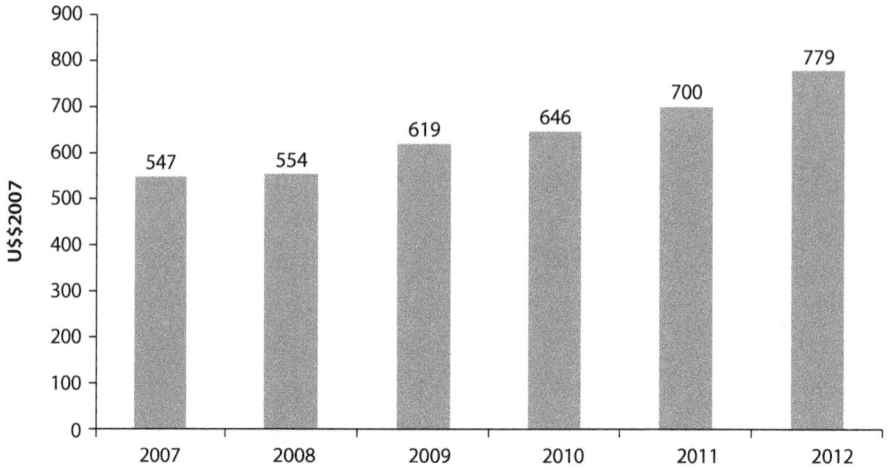

Source: World Bank SSEIR/ICEFI social spending database.

Figure 5.8 Average Test Results, Third Grade, El Salvador

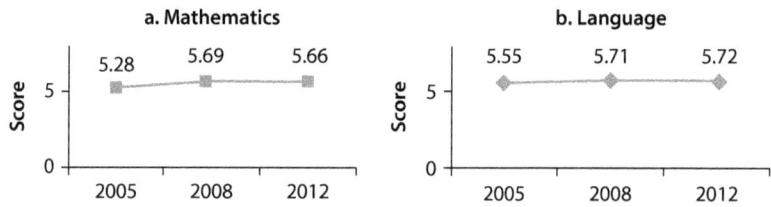

Source: Prueba de Aprendizajes y Aptitudes para Egresados de Educación Básica (National Assessment of Learning Competencies for Basic Education Graduates).

Figure 5.9 Upper Secondary Learning Outcomes Compared with per-Student Spending, El Salvador

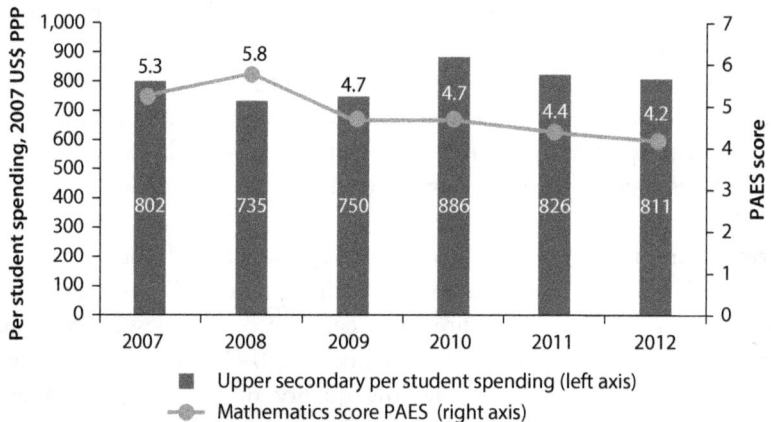

Sources: World Bank SSEIR/ICEFI social spending database; EdStats; official data in "Aspectos Institucionales del Sector de Educación de El Salvador."
Note: PAES = Learning and Skills Test for Graduates of Secondary Education.

to other Latin American countries, as is the wage bill as a percentage of public education spending. However, the profile of the teachers and the quality of in service training is generally reduced. Furthermore, generally countries have reduced incentives for teachers to significantly improve their performance as there is reduced accountability or pay-for-performance, and there are few competency tests to screen teacher candidates. In addition, the subregion is characterized by high rates of teacher absenteeism.

A recent evaluation of a doubling of teacher wages in Indonesia provides an example outside of Latin America of how higher wages are not sufficient to improve performance. De Ree et al. (2015) analyze a large-scale randomized experiment across a representative sample of Indonesian schools. They find that a doubling of pay led to increased teacher satisfaction with their jobs and less teacher stress, but that after two or three years it had not led to improvements in measures of teacher effort or student learning outcomes.

Honduras provides a Central American example where high teacher salaries are even associated with poor education outcomes. Teacher salaries are high in Honduras compared to other LAC countries (figure 5.10). As a result, the wage bill, accounting for almost 90 percent of total public spending on education in Honduras, is strikingly high compared to similar countries.[5] The share of expenditures going to salaries is also much higher than countries with first-rate education systems, such as Finland and the Republic of Korea. In 2012, only 2 percent of the total public spending on education went to construction, renovation, rehabilitation, and nonroutine maintenance of facilities.

Figure 5.10 Teacher Salaries in Relation to GDP per Capita, LAC, circa 2010

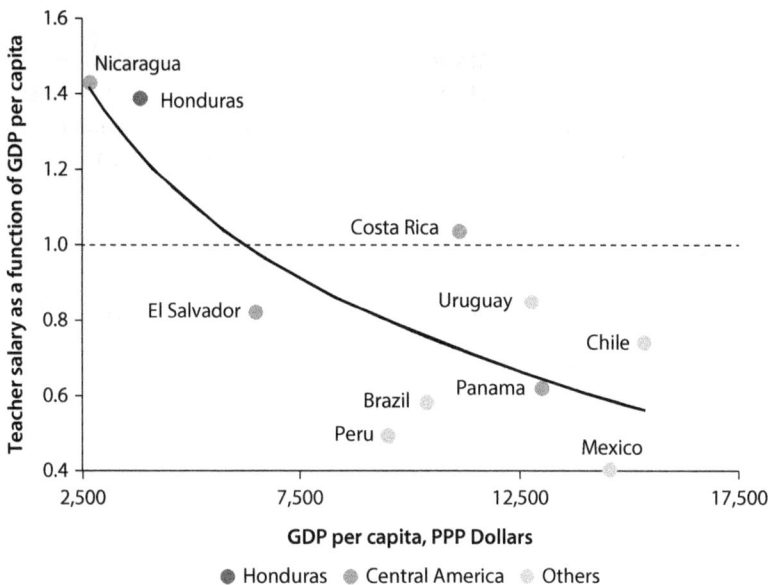

Sources: Teacher salary data from household survey data compiled by World Bank; GDP in PPP terms from World Bank Atlas, in Bruns and Luque (2014).

The picture is similar for higher education. Between 2008 and 2011, the share of wages averaged 83 percent of total higher education expenditures. Yet, Honduran students underperform in language, mathematics, and science tests compared to those in other countries. Evidence from TIMSS and the Progress in International Reading Literacy Study (PIRLS) confirms the insights from the national standardized tests that Honduran students are performing at very low levels (figure 5.2–5.4). Even though 4th grade tests were applied to 6th graders in Honduras, by recommendation of the TIMSS and PIRLS International Study Center, Honduran 6th graders ranked very low in 4th grade TIMSS mathematics examinations compared to other countries (figures 5.11 and 5.12). Likewise, despite applying the 8th grade test to 9th graders in Honduras, results in 8th grade TIMSS mathematics were comparatively even lower (figure 5.13).

In addition, there is evidence that these poor learning results in 2011 in Honduras are due to a combination of factors, including a low number of school days and actual learning time. The official school year in Honduras should be at least 200 days, but it is often disrupted by teacher strikes and demonstrations. Teachers represent about half of all civil servants and are the group most easily organized for political action. They are therefore a strong political group in Honduran politics and important beneficiaries of distributional politics. The teachers' union pushes an agenda that defends their interests, often sacrificing equality of educational opportunity (box 5.1). According to data from the Secretaría de Estado en el Despacho de Educación (Ministry of Education; SEDUC), schools were closed about a third of the days they were supposed to be open (on average for 2002–11). For instance, in 2011, 60 of the 200 school days were lost.[6]

Figure 5.11 TIMSS 2011 Mathematics Fourth Grade (Sixth Grade for Honduras) and GDP per Capita

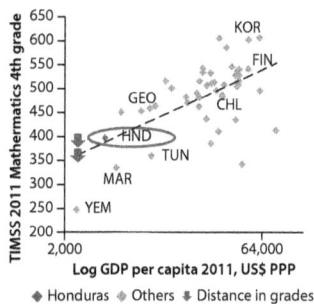

◆ Honduras ◆ Others ↓ Distance in grades

Sources: TIMSS 2011 Assessment; EdStats.
Note: CHL = Chile; FIN = Finland; GEO = Georgia; HND = Honduras; KOR = Republic of Korea; MAR = Morocco; PPP = purchasing power parity; TUN = Tunisia; YEM = Republic of Yemen.

Figure 5.12 PIRLS 2011 Fourth Grade (Sixth Grade for Honduras) and GDP per Capita

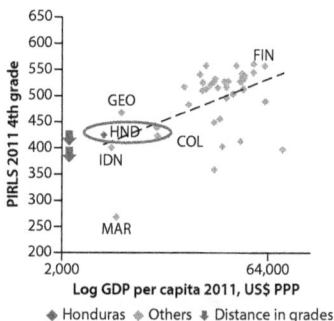

◆ Honduras ◆ Others ↓ Distance in grades

Sources: TIMSS 2011 Assessment; EdStats.
Note: COL = Colombia; FIN = Finland; GEO = Georgia; HND = Honduras; IDN = Indonesia; MAR = Morocco; PPP = purchasing power parity.

Figure 5.13 TIMSS 2011 Mathematics Eighth Grade (Sixth Grade for Honduras) and GDP per Capita

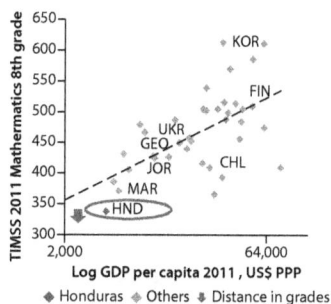

◆ Honduras ◆ Others ↓ Distance in grades

Sources: TIMSS 2011 Assessment; EdStats.
Note: CHL = Chile; FIN = Finland; GEO = Georgia; HND = Honduras; KOR = Republic of Korea; JOR = Jordan; MAR = Morocco; PPP = purchasing power parity; UKR = Ukraine.

Box 5.1 Politics Matter—Strong Teachers' Unions Often Fight Changes

Teachers' unions in LAC have a history of successfully defending their interests by being active in electoral politics, strikes, mobilization of public support, and legal action. Many reforms with the goal of improving educational quality may threaten the interests of teachers and unions.

Curriculum reforms, student testing, and teacher evaluation systems create changes to working conditions that teachers may find uncomfortable. Pay for performance, higher standards for teachers, and alternative certification requirements can threaten the pay and benefits of experienced teachers.

Local control of schools and school choice programs may diminish union bargaining power. The deepest challenge in raising teacher quality is not fiscal or technical, but political, because teachers' unions in every country in Latin America are large and politically active stakeholders (Bruns and Luque 2014).

The subregion has been innovating in some of these issues. For instance, recent reforms in El Salvador include mandatory teacher exams, full-time schooling, and school-based management (SBM). El Salvador is a widely regarded laboratory of school reform in the region. In 2000, the Government of El Salvador established a mandatory exam—the Evaluación de las Competencias Académicas y Pedagógicas (Evaluation of Academic Competencies and Pedagogy; ECAP)—for teachers exiting teacher pre-service training programs. Although the portion of teachers passing the ECAP has increased dramatically over time—from roughly 40 percent in 2001 to almost 80 percent in 2012—the teachers attending training programs represent a minority of the entire teaching corps so far. Further, the curriculum has not been linked to the traditions of the local culture and the needs of the local labor markets, thus creating a gap between the demand and supply of relevant skills.

The new full-time school (FTS) model in El Salvador builds on a strong territorial strategy to promote quality. As part of the territorial strategy, schools within a given municipality have been reorganized to form clusters, within which they share and are governed by a unique governance and administration system.[7] Each cluster of schools aims to provide a full set of school services, ranging from preschool to upper secondary levels. Besides the improved supply of school services, the FTS model promotes greater collaboration across schools, leveraging equipment, resources, teachers, and expertise within clusters.

More than the mere extension of the school day, the FTS reform focuses on new pedagogical approaches in the classroom to increase student learning, provide for the professionalization of the teaching career path, and install a more robust monitoring and evaluation information system. More time is allocated to learning, as the instructional time increases from 25 to 40 hours per week. The additional time is devoted to traditional subjects as well as to new ones,

Toward More Efficient and Effective Public Social Spending in Central America
http://dx.doi.org/10.1596/978-1-4648-1060-2

such as music, art, and crafts. The inclusion of additional subjects is part of a new and broader education model, valuing an extended set of competencies and values (such as citizenship). The contents and the pedagogical practice, unlike the previous model, are expected to be more in line with the characteristics of the surrounding community. The SBM program, Educación con Participación de la Comunidad (Education with Community Participation; EDUCO), which has been discontinued, achieved results in expanding coverage to rural areas and in reducing dropouts and teacher absenteeism.

Effectiveness and Efficiency of Health Services

There has been recent progress in health indicators in all Central American countries, but some challenges remain, especially in nutrition, maternal mortality, and noncommunicable diseases (NCDs), affirming the importance of allocating more resources toward preventive care and health promotion. Life expectancy rates improved in all the countries such that the average life expectancy in Central America increased from 73 years in 2007 to 75 years in 2014, which is equal to the LAC 2014 average and higher than the middle-income country 2014 average of 68 years.

The record on undernourishment, however is mixed, with improvements in Honduras and Panama but increases in undernourishment in El Salvador and Guatemala. Chronic malnutrition remains a significant problem, especially in Guatemala, where almost one out of two children under age 5 is stunted, and in Honduras, where slightly more than one in five children under age 5 is stunted.

All Central American countries have made progress in reducing child mortality rates and maternal mortality ratios (MMRs), although all of them were more successful in decreasing the former than the latter. El Salvador, in particular, reached its Millennium Development Goal for child mortality, but not for maternal mortality. However, its MMR (69 per 100,000 births) is lower than the LAC average (71 per 100,000 births). Most health indicators are better in Costa Rica than in any other Central American country and are comparable to health indicators in countries with much higher incomes. In general, health indicators in Costa Rica are better than the LAC average, while in the rest of Central America health indicators are worse than the LAC average. There has been little improvement in Costa Rica in recent years because, despite its middle-income status, most of its indicators are already comparable to those in high-income countries and therefore there is less room for improvement.

Aging populations also create more health challenges, and NCDs (for example, heart ailments, hypertension, diabetes, and cancers) have emerged as among the leading causes of deaths in all Central American countries. In particular, chronic diseases pose a major threat to Costa Rica's health system due to a surge in demand for medical care and increasing costs (box 5.2). While there is a need to provide medical care to people who already have chronic diseases, it will be important to understand the drivers of cost and to implement cost-effective methods of managing these cases. In addition, reducing the incidence of these

Box 5.2 Challenges Posed by NCDs to the Costa Rican Health System

NCDs pose the greatest challenge to Costa Rica's health care system. Improvements in income, environment, lifestyles, and medical services have resulted in higher life expectancy and a rapid increase in the number of elderly as a percentage of the population (figure B5.2.1, panels A and B), leading to a rise in chronic and other noncommunicable diseases and greater demand for long-term care. The increased demand introduces new pressures including clinical (new diseases that require new treatments), financial (escalating costs and continuous use of the health system over time), and those related to patient satisfaction. As a result, the country's health care and financial administrative management model shows signs of stress, as suggested by patient dissatisfaction, mainly because of waiting lists.

Figure B5.2.1 Demographic Trends in Costa Rica, 1990 Compared with 2005

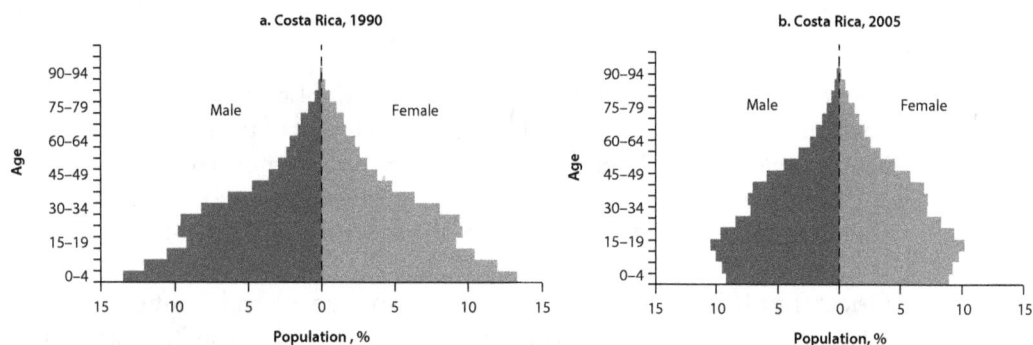

Source: WHO: Country Basic Data 2013.

diseases (new cases) will be more cost-effective. However, most Central American countries tend to allocate the largest share of their budgets to curative care, especially to hospitals. Moreover, not all countries in Central America have included NCD prevention and control as part of their primary basic package. Guatemala recently included it in its new PHC model, but El Salvador has not. There is also the issue of addressing additional resource requirements and sustainability of existing NCD prevention programs, such as in Panama.

Human resources are the most important health input, yet lack of health care personnel remains a major quality constraint in most Central American countries. Four of the Central American countries that we study have much lower ratios of health personnel to population than the WHO-recommended 25 per 10,000 inhabitants (figure 5.14). Guatemala has the lowest ratio of health personnel to population (12.5 per 10,000 inhabitants) in Central America. Furthermore, human resources tend to be disproportionately distributed in urban areas compared to rural areas. Even Panama, which has an overall ratio of health personnel to population that is greater than the WHO guidelines, has significant human

Figure 5.14 Health Worker Ratios per 10,000 Inhabitants

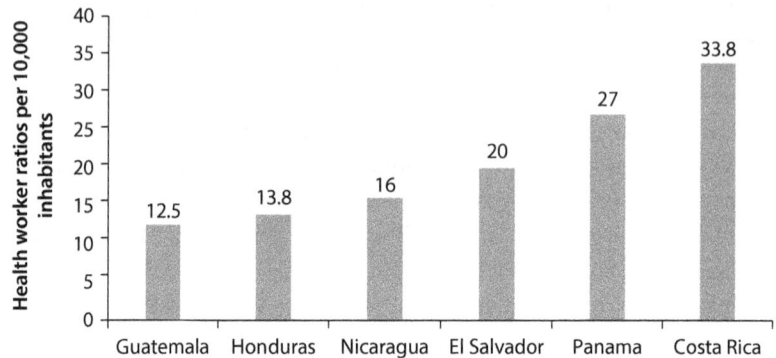

Source: Pan American Health Organization (PAHO) and Consejo de Ministros de Salud de Centroamérica (COMISCA) Human Resources Observatory website 2013. http://www.observatoriorh.org/centro/.

resource gaps in rural and indigenous areas. Only 11.6 percent of doctors and 15.7 percent of nurses are in rural areas, yet 35 percent of the population is rural, and Panama City has 74 percent of medical specialists in the country.

Access to medicines and supplies remains an issue in some Central American countries. In Guatemala, in June 2015, the average availability of drugs was 87 percent for all 29 health directorates, ranging from 66 percent (Petén Sur Oriente) to 100 percent (Santa Rosa and Totonicapan), and 7 out of 44 hospitals had less than 75 percent drug availability. In Honduras, in 2012 and 2013, serious drug shortages led the government to make emergency purchases of medicines to meet the pressing needs in major health centers and hospitals. In El Salvador, health facilities report a lack of medical supplies, as well as the slow replacement of equipment. The assessment of the delays in achieving Millennium Development Goal 5 (reducing maternal mortality) identified the lack of supplies as having a direct impact on the services provided to pregnant women during institutional delivery.

The share of the population that is very satisfied or satisfied with public hospitals is higher in Central America than the average for seven LAC countries. Because hospitals comprise the largest share of public health spending among health programs, user satisfaction with hospitals is an important indicator of quality. From 2007 to 2011, overall satisfaction with hospitals (figure 5.15) significantly increased from 53 percent to 72 percent in Nicaragua. Although it also increased in Guatemala, it remains low at 46 percent. Satisfaction rates decreased in Costa Rica, Panama, and Honduras. The average overall satisfaction rate (59 percent) for Central American countries is higher than the average (40 percent) for seven comparator countries[8] in the region.

Use of private health care may indicate low quality among public health care facilities. If the quality of public health care is low, then there is an incentive to pay for private care. If private health care spending is high, this is likely to be an

Figure 5.15 Would You Say You Are Satisfied with the Way the Public Hospitals Work?

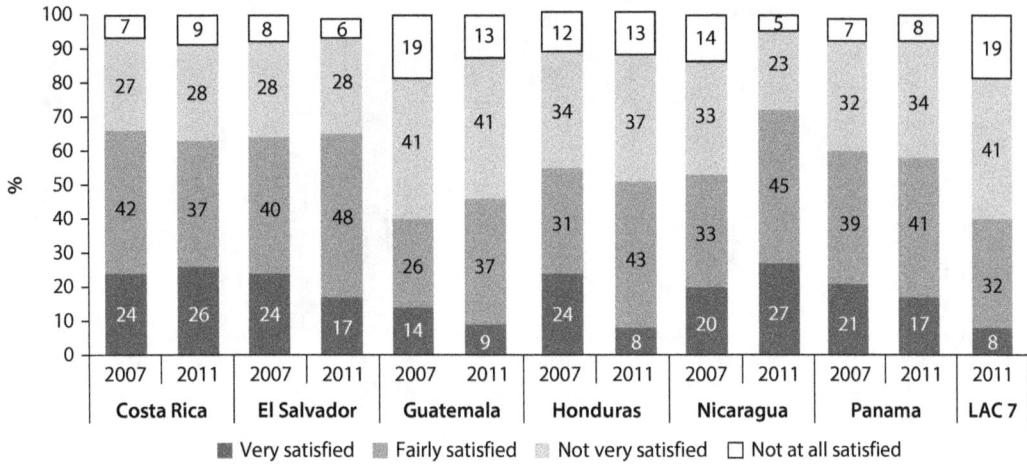

Source: World Bank calculations using Latinobarómetro.
Note: LAC 7 = Argentina, Brazil, Chile, Colombia, Ecuador, Mexico, and Peru.

indication that public health care is of low quality, particularly in countries where free health care is provided in public facilities. In El Salvador, Guatemala, and Honduras, but not in Costa Rica, the rich are more likely to use private health care. In all countries, a majority of the health care provided to the first four income quintiles is in public facilities. In Guatemala, Honduras, and Panama, private facilities provide the majority of health care to the top income quintiles, while in Costa Rica and El Salvador, a majority of the upper and top income quintiles use public facilities (figure 5.16–5.18). In Costa Rica, in particular, the use of public facilities across all income quintiles remains very high (at least 80 percent) even though the share of private health spending has increased. In fact, inpatient use of public facilities is highest for the highest-income quintile (93 percent; figure 5.18).

In terms of spending, the share of private health care spending in total health care spending is lower than the LAC average in Costa Rica, El Salvador, Nicaragua, and Panama, but higher than the LAC average in Guatemala and Honduras (figure 5.19). However, the out-of-pocket share of private spending on health in Central America is 85.9 percent, which is higher than the LAC average of 68 percent. Guatemala has the lowest public spending share on health (38 percent) despite the provision of free health care in public facilities. In Panama and Costa Rica, the private health care share of total health spending has increased, although the use of public facilities remains high (at least 70 percent) for the first four income quintiles in the former and in all income quintiles (at least 80 percent) in the latter.

Still, even in Costa Rica the quality of health care is perceived to be declining (that is, long waiting lines), while private services are well regarded.

Figure 5.16 Use of Public and Private Health Care Facilities, by Quintile, Guatemala and Panama, 2008

a. Guatemala

b. Panama

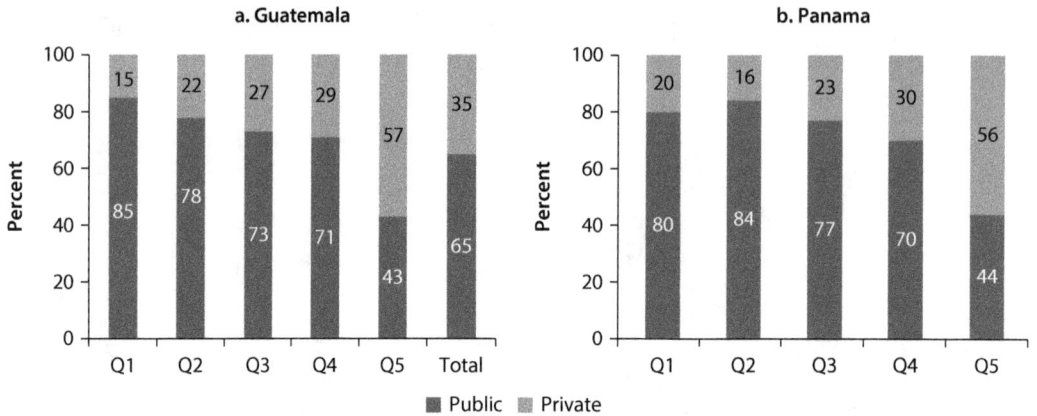

Source: World Bank analysis of household surveys; calculations using standardized ADePT Software (Health Module).

Source: World Bank analysis of household surveys; calculations using Encuesta de Niveles de Vida (ENV) 2008.

Figure 5.17 Use of Public and Private Outpatient Services and Hospitals, by Quintile, El Salvador, 2013

a. Outpatient services

b. Hospitalization

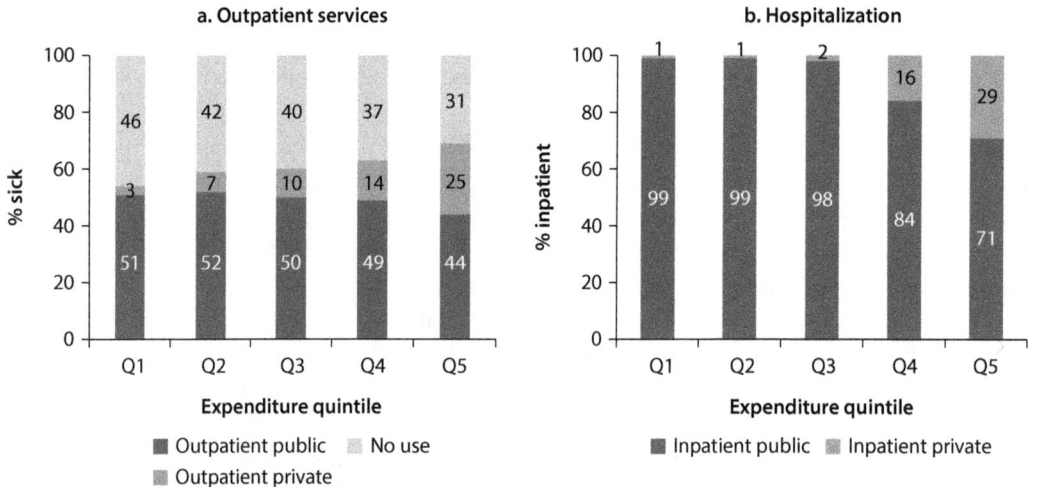

Source: World Bank analysis of household surveys; calculations using standardized ADePT Software (Health Module).

In El Salvador, the private health care shares of spending decreased, which is likely related to the removal of fees in public health facilities. In Honduras, the private health care shares of total health spending decreased during 2007–13, from 54 percent to 51 percent, and in Guatemala, from 67 percent to 62 percent, but remained high.

In terms of service delivery and governance of the health system, fragmentation and lack of coordination among major health institutions result in duplication of efforts and inefficiencies in the sector. In most countries in

Figure 5.18 Patient Visits, by Quintile, Costa Rica, 2006

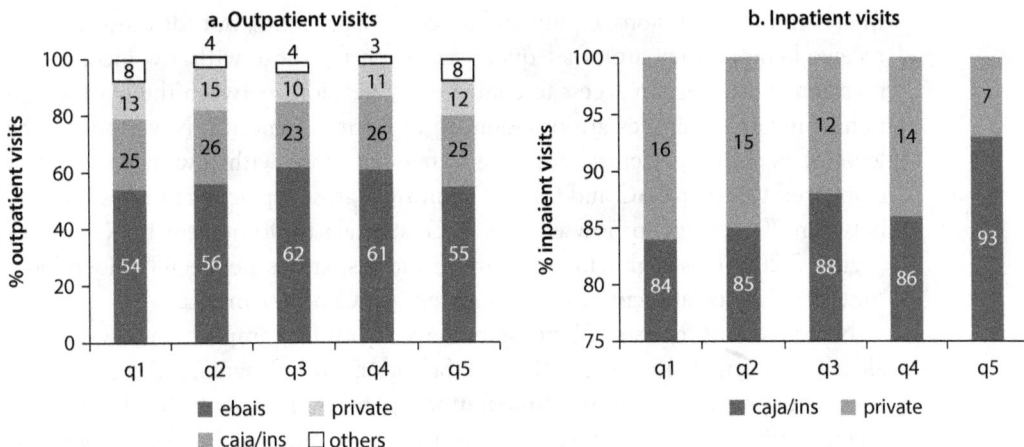

a. Outpatient visits

| | ebais | private |
| caja/ins | others |

b. Inpatient visits

| caja/ins | private |

Source: World Bank analysis of household surveys; calculations using standardized ADePT software (Health Module).

Figure 5.19 Public-Private Spending Shares of Total Health Spending, 2013

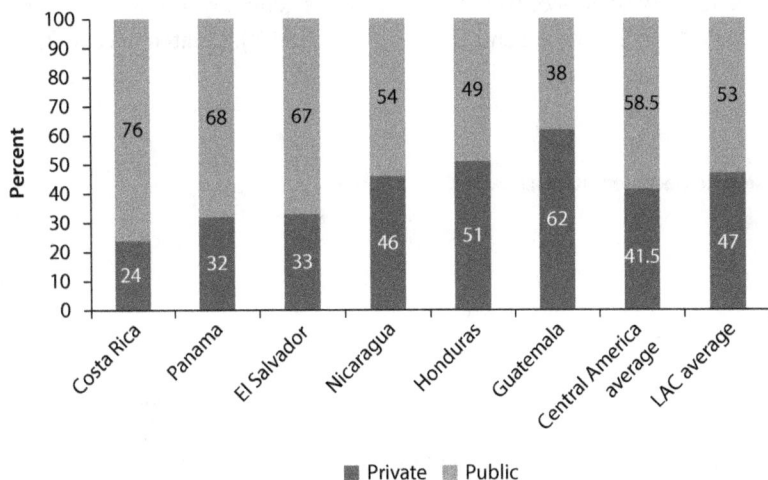

Private   Public

Source: World Bank, *World Development Indicators 2015.*

Central America, there is insufficient coordination among key public health institutions such as the Ministry of Health and the Social Security Institute, contributing to duplication of services in a number of areas and inefficiencies in the procurement of medicines and supplies. Fragmentation also results in the provision of different packages of services that depend on affiliation with a particular type of social health insurance regime or whether a person is covered by the MOH. These issues, together with challenges related to sector budgeting, monitoring, and implementing accountability mechanisms, are discussed further in chapter 6.

Effectiveness and Efficiency of Social Protection and Labor Spending

In contributory pensions, equity and access remain issues, but for those who do receive benefits they are of adequate size, even for those with low incomes. As mentioned, the gaps in access to contributory pensions between the poorest and richest income quintiles are pronounced in Central America. Nevertheless, the level of benefits in Central America is fair for those with low incomes when compared to other LAC and OECD countries (gross replacement rates oscillate between 70 percent for low earners in Guatemala to 90 percent in Nicaragua) (figure 5.20). This highlights even more the disparities between "insiders" and "outsiders" in social security pension systems in Central America.

Noncontributory (social) pensions have a positive impact on low-income elderly, especially in Costa Rica, El Salvador, and Panama. In those countries, the proportion of noncontributory pension recipients in the first or second quintiles is 72 percent in Costa Rica, 66 percent in El Salvador, and 54 percent in Panama (figure 5.21). Social pensions are less well targeted in Honduras and Guatemala; in Honduras, 49 percent of social pension recipients are in the top income quintile, and in Guatemala, 25 percent are in the top income quintile.

The generosity of noncontributory pensions is generally low. Most generous are Costa Rica (US$5.2 per day) and El Salvador (US$4.8). Guatemala and Nicaragua

Figure 5.20 Gross Pension Replacement Rates: Low and High Earners

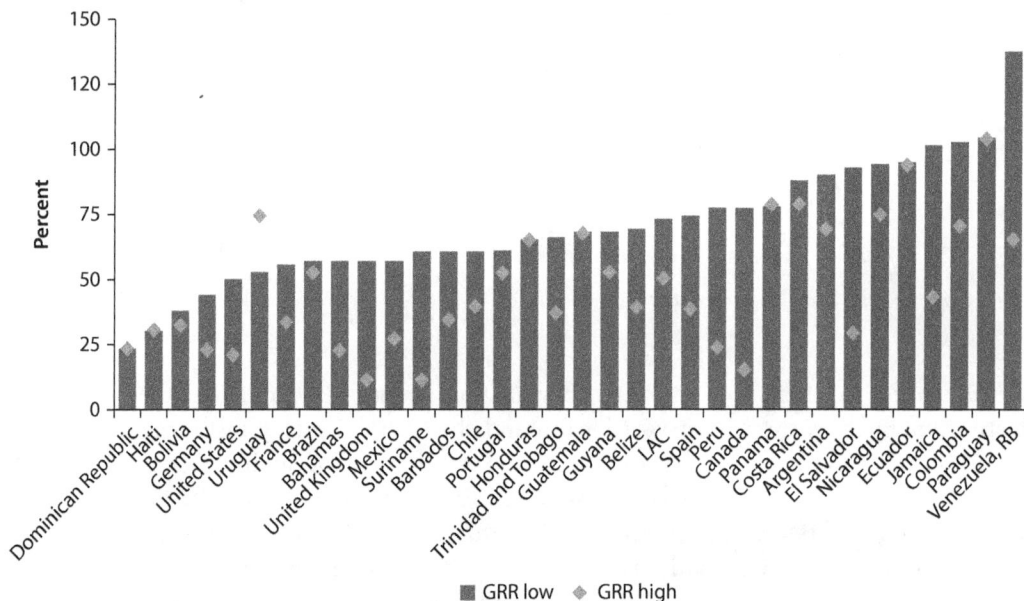

■ GRR low   ◆ GRR high

Sources: OECD/Inter-American Development Bank/World Bank 2014.
Note: GRR = gross replacement rate.

Figure 5.21 Social Pension Distribution of Beneficiaries, by Quintile

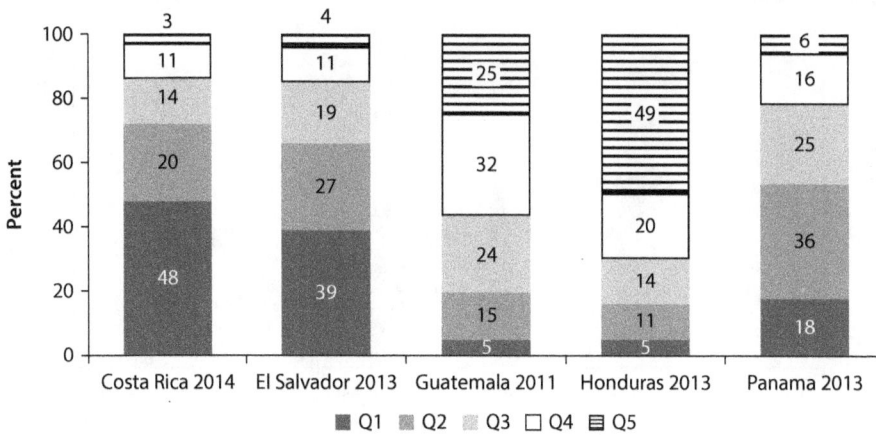

Source: World Bank SSEIR/ICEFI social spending database.

pay about US$0.5 per day. Honduras's payments are lowest (US$0.2 per day). Noncontributory pensions are well below the minimum wage in all Central American countries. The highest is in El Salvador, where noncontributory pension payments are 42.2 percent of the minimum wage. The lowest is in Honduras, where noncontributory pension payments are only 1.4 percent of the minimum wage (figure 5.22).

An aging population will lead to more beneficiaries and fewer contributors to pension coffers, resulting in sustainability challenges for both contributory and social pensions. The aging population is a particular problem because pensions are financed through payroll taxes, which fewer people will pay as an increasing proportion of the population retires.

Conditional cash transfer (CCT) programs have had a significant positive impact on poverty (figure 5.23), educational attainment, and health status. CCTs are probably the most evaluated type of social program in the world, and the evidence is overwhelming that these programs increase human capital accumulation through more access to health and education services (Fiszbein and Schady 2009). Central American CCTs are not an exception, with impact evaluations performed across all countries, including an earlier experience in Nicaragua with *Red de Protección Social*, a program later discontinued.

In Guatemala, a difference-in-differences evaluation of Mi Familia Progresa (My Family Progresses, MIFAPRO, the predecessor to *Mi Bono Seguro*) identified enrollment increases of 8.6 percent, 10.9 percent, and 11 percent for the first, second, and third levels of primary. In Honduras, a randomized controlled trial evaluation of Bono 10,000 (now renamed as *Bono Vida Mejor*) in rural areas identified an increase in per capita consumption by seven percent, primary school enrollment increased by 2.8 percentage points, and visits to health

Figure 5.22 Social Pensions in Central America: Monthly Payment per Day and Share of Minimum Wage, 2012

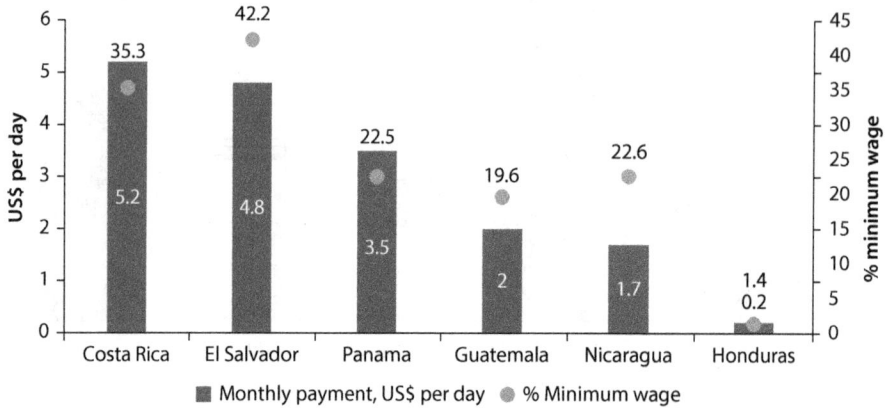

Source: World Bank calculations based on in-country legislative minimum wages.

Figure 5.23 Social Assistance Programs—Important Positive Impact of CCTs on Extreme Poverty among Beneficiaries

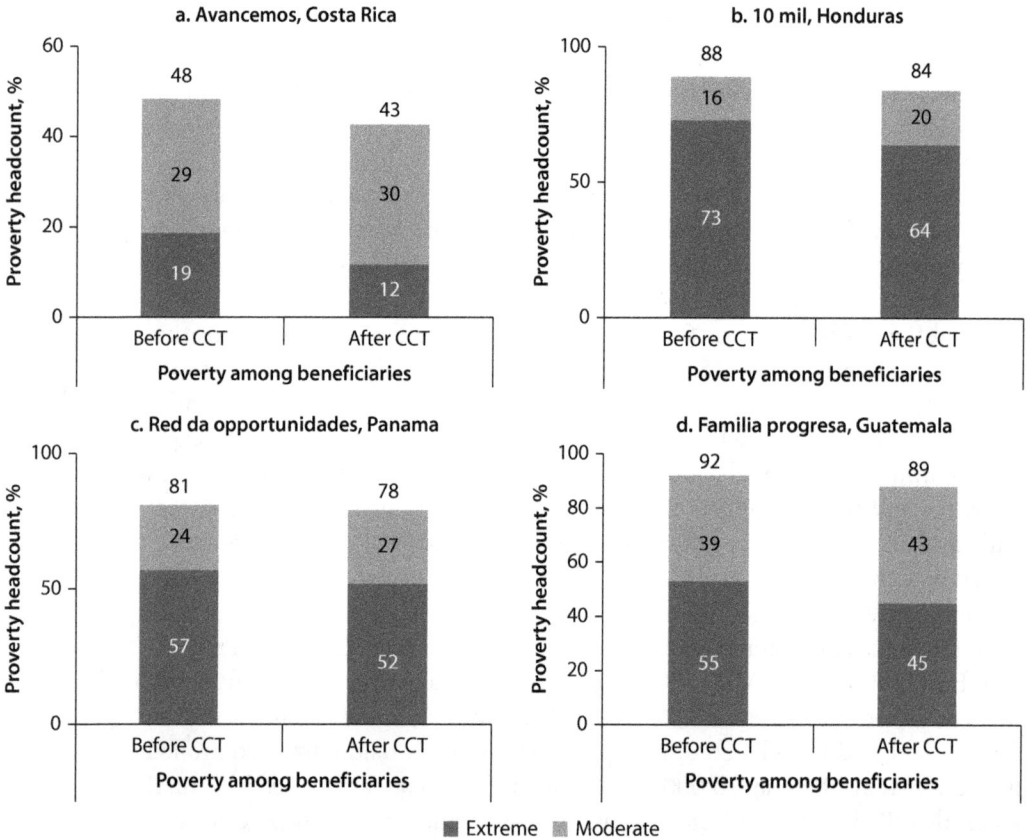

Source: World Bank analysis of household surveys; calculations using standardized ADePT Software (Social Protection Module).

centers for children age 0–3 increased by 2.6 percentage points (NORC-University of Chicago 2013). Preliminary analysis suggests that *Avancemos* in Costa Rica has had an impact on poverty and secondary school enrollment. Estimates using 2014 household survey data and national poverty lines showed that the CCTs seem to have reduced the extreme poverty and total poverty headcounts by 0.4 percentage points nationwide. Moreover, estimates show that the CCTs have an impact on enrollment and attendance, especially at the upper secondary level (box 5.3).

Enrollment rates at the upper secondary level are higher among children who benefit from the program than among those that did not receive the benefit. In Nicaragua, an evaluation based on a randomized, community-based intervention with measurements before and after the intervention in both treatment and control communities of the Social Protection Network (Red de Protección Social) pilot identified an increase in primary school enrollment rates by nearly 13 percentage points (box 5.4). In Panama, preliminary analysis suggests that the CCT *Red de Oportunidades* almost doubled enrollment in primary and secondary schools for program participants, reduced acute diarrheal disease and acute respiratory infection in children under age 5, and increased prenatal care visits. It can also be attributed with a reduction of 2.3 percentage points in total poverty and 5.1 percentage points in extreme poverty among beneficiaries.

Box 5.3 Impact of Avancemos CCT in Costa Rica

The *Avancemos* CCT program was launched in 2006 with the objective of promoting the retention and reintegration into the formal education system of children from families struggling to keep their children in secondary school. From 2006 to 2015, the government increased the cash transfer in accordance with the grade completed, so that the incentive to stay in school is greater at higher grades. Since 2015, there have been only two categories of benefit amount: 22,500 colones for 7th to 9th grades (lower secondary) and 35,000 colones for 10th to 12th grades (upper secondary). The transfer is paid monthly provided the student remains in the educational system. The coverage expanded from 8,137 students in 2006 to 185,314 in 2011 and then declined to 174,196 in 2014.

Evaluations of *Avancemos* find that it had a significant impact on secondary school dropout and reinsertion in Costa Rica. One evaluation using panel data, propensity score matching, and difference-in-differences analysis found that *Avancemos* decreased dropout rates by 10–16 percent per year and had a statistically significant positive impact on the reinsertion rates of those who had dropped out (Mata and Hernández 2015).

Figure B5.3.1 illustrates changes in enrollment as a result of the program. Enrollment rates at the upper secondary level are higher among children who benefited from the program than among those who did not receive the benefit. Moreover, estimates using the 2014 household survey data and national poverty lines showed that *Avancemos* seems to have reduced the extreme poverty and total poverty headcounts by 0.4 percentage points nationwide.

box continues next page

Box 5.3 Impact of Avancemos CCT in Costa Rica *(continued)*

Figure B5.3.1 Enrollment Rates, Ages 5–20, Costa Rica, 2014 (Extreme Poor)

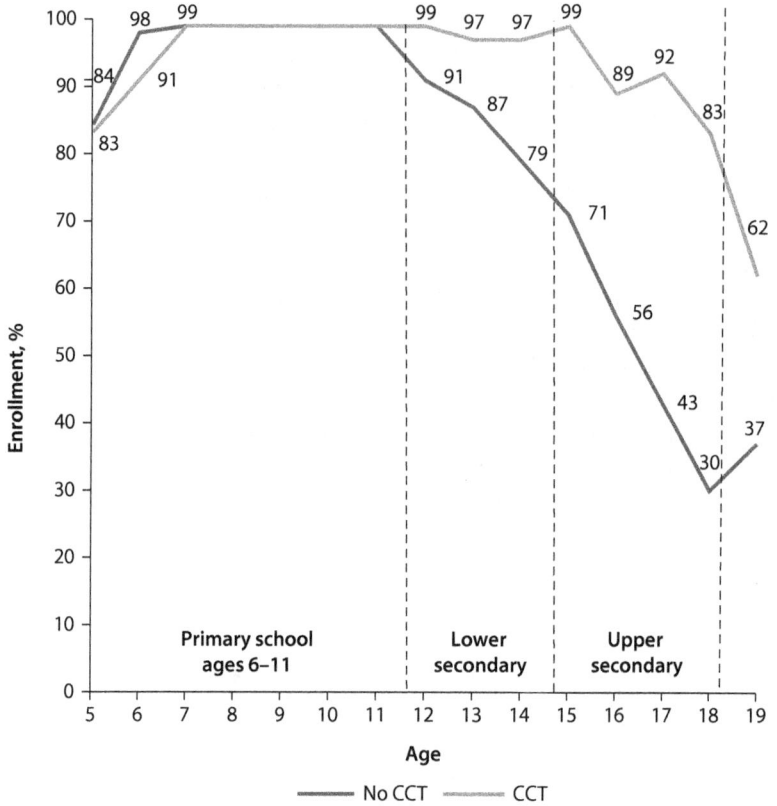

Source: World Bank calculations based on analysis of household surveys.

Box 5.4 The Experience of the *Red de Protección Social* CCT in Nicaragua

Unlike all other countries in Central America and more than 60 countries in the world, Nicaragua does not have a CCT or unconditional cash transfer in place (though *Programa Amor* provides some cash in exchange for attendance at community workshops in certain areas). However, from 2000 to 2006, it had one of the first CCTs in the world, called *Red de Protección Social*. This program was discontinued by the new administration in 2007, when there was a change in focus in terms of social assistance and social care.

Red de Protección Social targeted poor households with children age 7–13 enrolled in primary school grades 1–4, and children age 0–5 attending health care services. It reached 36,000 households during its existence. The Emergency Social Investment Fund implemented it.

box continues next page

Box 5.4 The Experience of the *Red de Protección Social* CCT in Nicaragua *(continued)*

The program has been thoroughly evaluated and it is frequently cited as the CCT with the highest impact in terms of poverty reduction, increase in consumption levels, and use of services. For instance, it was estimated that the program: reduced poverty incidence by 5–10 percentage points and reduced extreme poverty by 15–20 percentage points, increased per capita consumption by 21–29 percent; increased enrollment among 7–13-year-old children by 12.8 percentage points (from a baseline of 72 percent); and increased the likelihood that children age 0–3 were weighed at a health center every six months by 13.1 percentage points (from a baseline of 55.4 percent).

Sources: Fiszbein and Schady 2009; Maluccio and Flores 2005.

Problems with CCT programs relate to transparency, targeting, and generosity. One study highlighted a number of shortcomings in the implementation of the *Mi Bono Seguro* CCT in Guatemala, especially related to lack of transparency in the selection of beneficiaries that were hampering the effectiveness of MIFAPRO. It also highlights the need to improve its targeting systems and monitoring and evaluation processes. In addition, in some countries generosity is low (figure 5.24).

ALMPs in Central America, especially training and apprenticeship programs, have not been successful in improving employment opportunities or wages for priority groups (that is, the young unemployed, the low skilled). For example, although Costa Rica spends more on ALMPs (as a percentage of GDP) than many OECD countries (figure 5.25), the performance of the largest ALMP in Costa Rica is disappointing. In Costa Rica, the Instituto Nacional de Aprendizaje (National Apprentice Institute; INA) accounts for the largest share in ALMPs by providing technical training (figure 5.26). Estimates show that returns to INA training are below those in private training programs and may even be negative (figure B5.5.1).

In general, little is known about the impact of most ALMP interventions. An exception is El Salvador's Programa de Apoyo Temporal al Ingreso (Temporary Income Support Program; PATI), a flagship government intervention that combines public works with technical training to the poor and low-skilled population (prioritizing youngsters and female household heads). The PATI has shown important (albeit in general short-lived) effects reducing extreme poverty among beneficiaries, increasing labor force participation and labor incomes, and improving readiness to start a new job (box 5.5).

The key lesson of programs such as the PATI is that ALMP interventions targeted to the low skilled should provide an appropriate package of services for the population facing different barriers or constraints to participation in the labor market, and should go beyond the one-size-fits-all approach by profiling the participants and providing service to them according to their need. In a new

Figure 5.24 Generosity of CCTs in Honduras, Panama, Costa Rica, and Guatemala

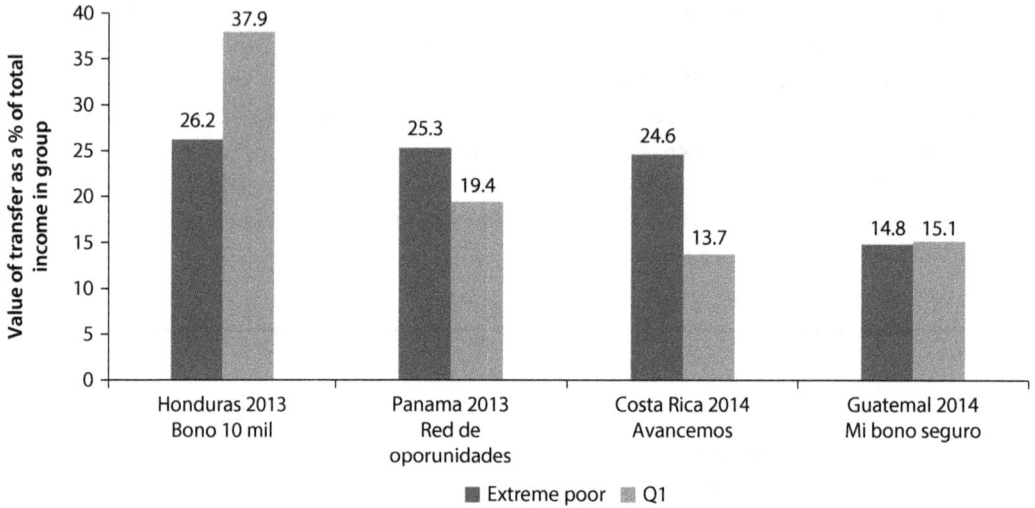

Source: World Bank SSEIR/ICEFI social spending database. Q1 = Lowest Income Quintile.

Figure 5.25 Public Spending on ALMPs as a Share of GDP

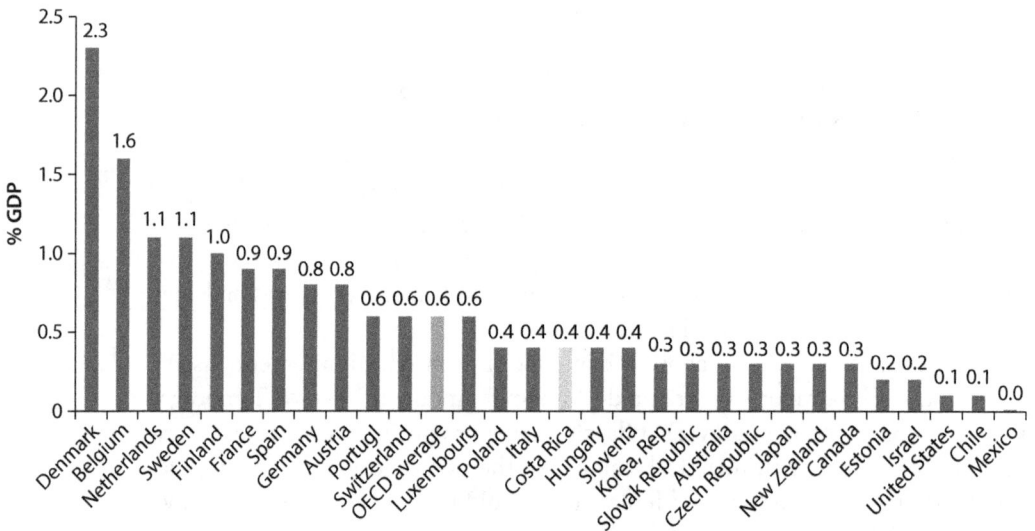

Source: OECD.

program to be launched in 2016 called *Jovenes Es Todo*, El Salvador is trying to build on the PATI to create a more comprehensive multi-intervention approach combining socioemotional and technical training, micro-entrepreneurship support, second chance education, and public works for youngsters with different problem and challenges.

Figure 5.26 Premium to Training Education, Costa Rica, 2009–14

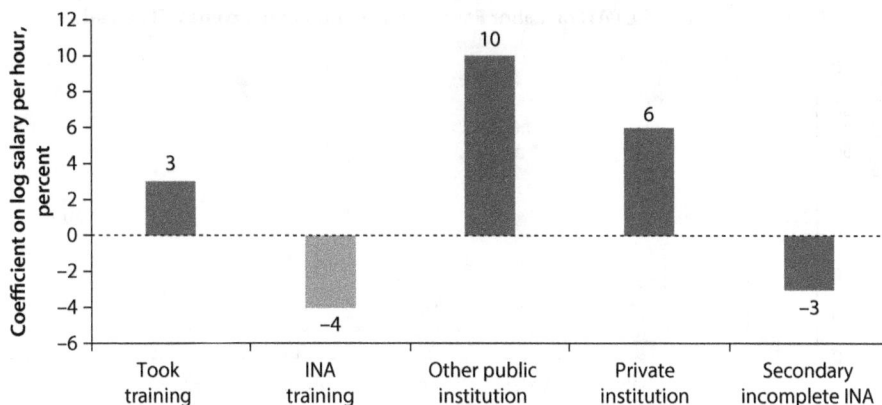

Source: World Bank calculations based on household surveys.
Note: Estimates use data from the household survey for 20–30-year-olds living with a parent, controlling for parents' education and income. Regressions do not control for self-selection. The numbers presented are the percentage difference between the wages of workers with each type of training and the wages of workers with no training. For example, a negative 4 percent implies a negative premium (a penalty) for INA training compared to no training.

Box 5.5 The Experience of the PATI in El Salvador

In El Salvador, the main ALMP intervention is the Programa de Apoyo Temporal al Ingreso (Temporary Income Support Program; PATI), a workfare program that combines income support with training. It is the core ALMP intervention in urban areas, benefiting about 63,000 participants so far in urban poor settlements in 36 municipalities. It has demonstrated positive impacts.

The PATI initially started as a response to the economic crisis affecting the country in 2009. It is aimed at mitigating poverty and improving productive capacities and enhanced opportunities for employment of female heads of household and youth. To achieve these goals, the PATI provides a cash benefit of US$100 per month for a maximum of six months, conditional on participation in community projects, occupational training, and labor market orientation courses. The expectation is that by the end of the six-month period, the beneficiaries can enter the labor market, create their own productive income generation activities, or both, to avoid being stuck in the vicious circle of poverty.

The lead implementing institution is the Social Investment Fund for Local Development. It coordinates with the following: municipalities, which formulate and monitor projects; the Ministry of Labor, which provides labor market orientation; and the Institute for Professional Training (INSAFORP), the national training institute, which is in charge of providing occupational training in areas selected according to local labor demand and participant profiles. In a rigorous evaluation, the PATI has already demonstrated positive impacts, including reducing extreme poverty among beneficiaries, increasing labor force participation and labor incomes (particularly among youth), and improving readiness to start a new job.

box continues next page

Box 5.5 The Experience of the PATI in El Salvador *(continued)*

Figure B5.5.1 Impact of the PATI on Labor Force Participation and Incomes, El Salvador

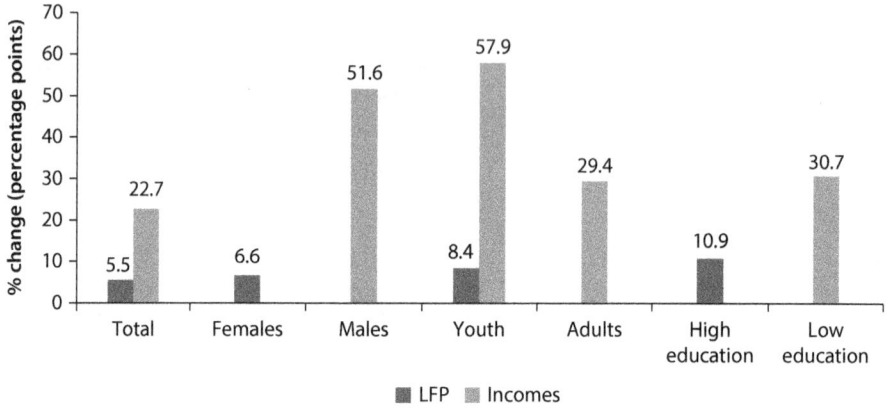

Source: Beneke de Sanfeliu and Acosta 2014.
Note: Impact corresponds to one year after program participation.

Cost-Effectiveness of Public Spending: Relating Spending to Outcome

Comparing the efficiency and cost-effectiveness of public social spending can shed light on the role of increasing the level of spending compared to redistributing existing spending to improve human development.[9] If public social spending is efficient and cost-effective, that indicates that the country is doing its best with available public resources. If social sector outcomes are low in countries where spending is efficient, that is an indication that to increase human development outcomes, the level of spending must increase. In countries where human development outcomes and cost-effectiveness are high, but efficiency is low, improving the efficiency of public social spending might have a bigger impact on human development than increasing the level of spending.

Only in Panama is overall public spending in the social sectors both efficient and moderately effective. Figure 5.27, panels A–D compare levels of public sector performance (PSP) and public sector efficiency (PSE) in countries in Central America and in other LAC countries. The PSP is a composite indicator based on socioeconomic variables that are assumed to be the output of public policies. This indicator summarizes the effectiveness of public spending in improving social outcomes. The PSE indicator then relates PSP scores to total public spending in these sectors. It represents the "public value" per public dollar spent (box 5.6 provides additional information on the PSP and PSE analyses). In Costa Rica, social spending is effective but inefficient. In Guatemala and Nicaragua, overall social spending is efficient but effectiveness is very low, leading to low PSP. In El Salvador and Honduras, overall social spending is neither efficient nor effective.

Figure 5.27 PSP and Efficiency in LAC, 2015

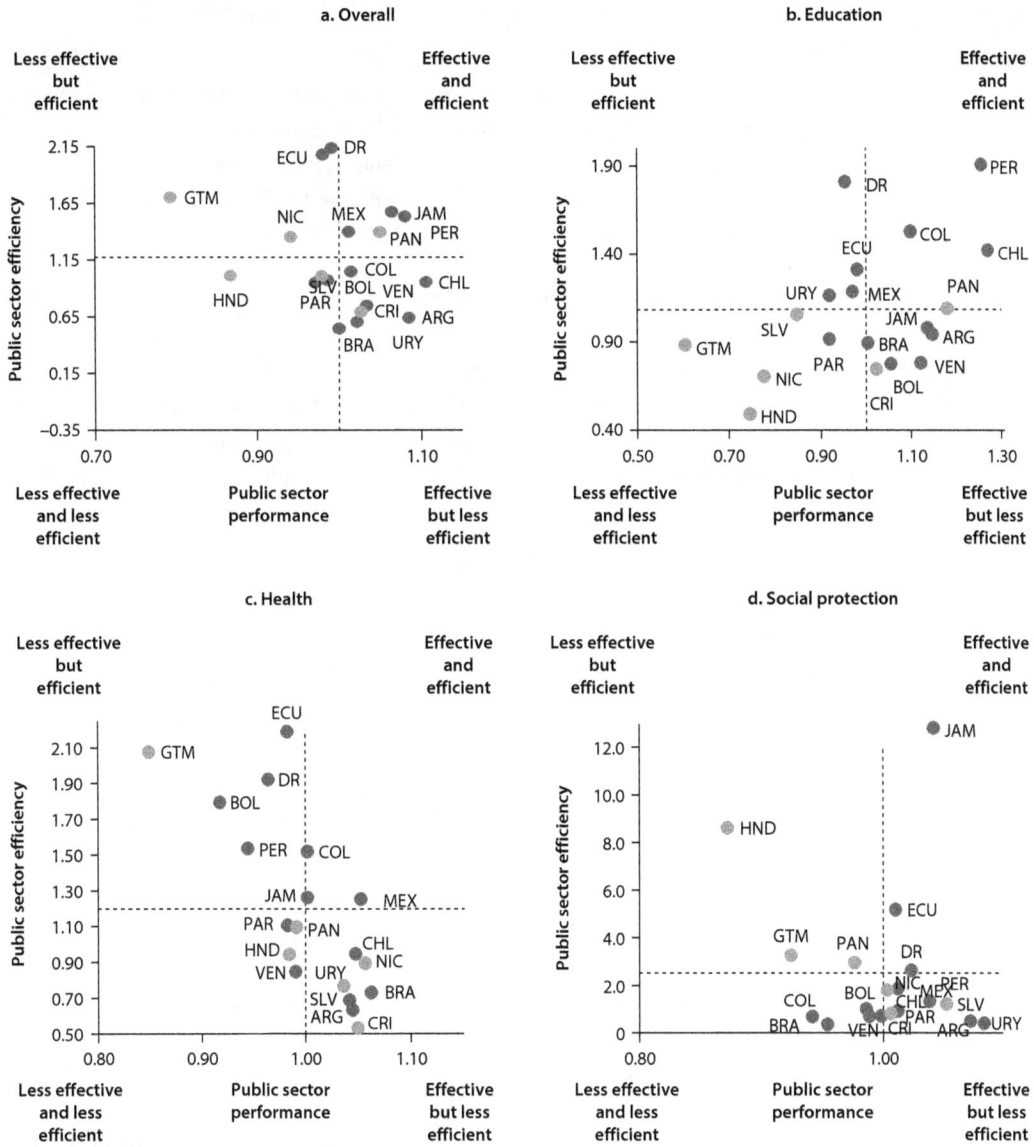

a. Overall

Less effective but efficient | Effective and efficient

Public sector efficiency

2.15 — ECU ● DR
1.65 — ● GTM
NIC MEX ●● JAM
1.15 — PAN PER
COL
HND SLV BOL VEN ● CHL
0.65 — PAR CRI ● ARG
BRA URY
0.15 —
−0.35 —

0.70   0.90   1.10

Less effective and less efficient | Public sector performance | Effective but less efficient

b. Education

Less effective but efficient | Effective and efficient

Public sector efficiency

1.90 — ● ● PER
DR
COL
ECU ●
1.40 — CHL
URY ● MEX PAN
SLV JAM
0.90 — ● GTM BRA ● ARG
NIC PAR VEN
BOL
CRI
0.40 — HND

0.50   0.70   0.90   1.10   1.30

Less effective and less efficient | Public sector performance | Effective but less efficient

c. Health

Less effective but efficient | Effective and efficient

Public sector efficiency

ECU
2.10 — ● GTM ●
1.90 — ● DR
BOL
1.70 —
1.50 — ● PER ● COL
1.30 — JAM ● ● MEX
1.10 — PAR ● PAN
HND ● CHL
0.90 — NIC
VEN ● URY
0.70 — SLV ● BRA
ARG ● CRI
0.50 —

0.80   0.90   1.00   1.10

Less effective and less efficient | Public sector performance | Effective but less efficient

d. Social protection

Less effective but efficient | Effective and efficient

Public sector efficiency

● JAM
12.0 —
10.0 —
● HND
8.0 —
6.0 — ● ECU
GTM PAN
4.0 — ● ● DR
NIC PER
2.0 — BOL MEX
COL CHL SLV
BRA VEN CRI PAR ARG URY
0 —

0.80   1.00

Less effective and less efficient | Public sector performance | Effective but less efficient

Source: World Bank calculations using CEPAL and World Development Indicators databases.
Note: ARG = Argentina; BOL = Bolivia; BRA = Brazil; CHL = Chile; COL = Colombia; CRI = Costa Rica; DR = ???; ECU = Ecuador; GTM = Guatemala; HND = Honduras; JAM = Jamaica; MEX = Mexico; NIC = Nicaragua; PAN = Panama; PAR = Paraguay; PER = Peru; SLV = El Salvador; URY = Uruguay; VEN = República Bolivariana de Venezuela.

Social spending is efficient but not effective in Guatemala and Nicaragua. This suggests that those countries, especially Guatemala, are efficiently using the resources available for the social sectors but that the level of social spending is inadequate. This problem is particularly noticeable in health in Guatemala, where the shares of public spending to GDP and per capita public spending on health are among the lowest in the LAC region (figure 5.27).

Toward More Efficient and Effective Public Social Spending in Central America
http://dx.doi.org/10.1596/978-1-4648-1060-2

Box 5.6 Public Sector Performance (PSP) and Public Sector Efficiency (PSE) Indicators

We analyzed the relationship between social outcomes and spending using the PSP and PSE approaches developed by Afonso, Schuknecht, and Tanzi (2005, 2010).[a] PSP is measured by constructing composite indicators based on observable social variables that are assumed to be the output of pursued social public policies. Specifically, the PSP for country $i = 1, \ldots, m$ with $j = 1, 2, 3$ social sectors (education, health, and SPL) is determined by

$$PSP_i = \sum_{j=1n} PSP_{ij}; \, i = 1, \ldots n; \; with \; PSP_{ij} = f\left(I_k\right), \, k = 1, \ldots, r. \tag{BV.7.1}$$

where $f(I_k)$ is a function of k observable social indicators (for education, we take gross secondary enrollment and literacy rate; for health, we take maternal mortality and immunization rates; and for social protection and labor (SPL), we take inequality [measured by the Gini coefficient] and extreme poverty headcount [percentage of population earning less than US$1.25 a day]).

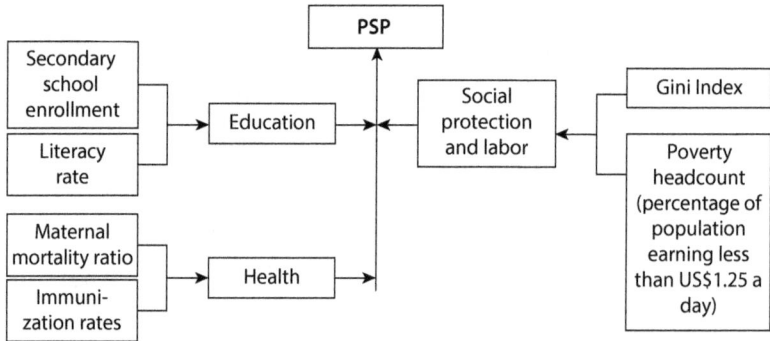

To obtain PSP indicators, we assign equal weight to each subindicator, computed as the average of the corresponding outcome indicators, each one normalized by its sample mean. The PSP indicator for each country is then obtained by averaging the values of all subindicators. Resulting PSP scores are then related to the average value of one of the normalized output indicators. Hence, countries with PSP scores in excess of 1 are viewed as good performers, while those countries with PSP values below the mean are not.

PSE relates PSP scores to their cost in terms of public spending. PSE weights PSP in each social sector by the amount of relevant public expenditure that is used to achieve such performance. To compute PSE scores, public spending in each sector is normalized across countries, taking the average value of 1 for each of the expenditure categories (EXP_{ij}). That is, for each country $i = 1, \ldots, m$ with $j = 1, 2, 3$ social sectors, the PSE is defined by

$$PSE_i = \sum_{j=1}^{n} \frac{PSP_{ij}}{EXP_{ij}}; \tag{BV.7.2}$$

a. The methodology follows Afonso, Schuknecht, and Tanzi (2005, 2010) for OECD countries, replicated later on in Afonso, Romero, and Monsalve (2013) for LAC.

At the opposite end of the spectrum from Guatemala and Nicaragua, social spending in Costa Rica is effective but not efficient. This suggests that increasing levels of social spending should not be the primary focus in Costa Rica so much as improving the efficiency of the high level of social spending. This conclusion is consistent with the earlier discussion on budget execution.

There is room for both increased efficiency and increased spending levels in social spending in Honduras. Social protection spending is efficient but not effective in Honduras while education and health spending are neither effective nor efficient.

Notes

1. Two comparable international standardized tests for primary school students have been implemented in many Central American countries: the Second Regional Comparative and Explanatory Study (SERCE) (2016) and the Third Regional Comparative and Explanatory Study (TERCE) (2013). SERCE and TERCE were large-scale studies of learning achievement in primary education in the LAC region. SERCE was administered in 2006 and tested mathematics and reading. TERCE, which was implemented in 2013, also tested mathematics and reading (plus writing [language] and natural sciences in 6th grade). Fifteen countries took part (Argentina, Brazil, Chile, Colombia, Costa Rica, the Dominican Republic, Ecuador, Guatemala, Honduras, Mexico, Nicaragua, Panama, Paraguay, Peru, and Uruguay), as well as the Mexican state of Nuevo Léon. The results allow learning achievements to be compared between pupils in the 3rd and 6th grades in the mathematics and reading tests for Costa Rica, Guatemala, El Salvador, Nicaragua, and Panama. A second OECD-administered worldwide standardized test, the Programme for International Student Assessment (PISA), implemented in 2009 and 2012, included only Costa Rica and Panama from Central America. As in the standardized tests discussed in the text, Panama performs worse that would be predicted by its GDP per capita and Costa Rica performs better. Costa Rica is included in 2009 and Panama in 2012, but the PISA web site does not present comparisons between 2009 and 2012 for either country.

2. Improvements in standardized test scores are supported by national assessments in Nicaragua but are not fully supported in Guatemala.

3. Falling returns in El Salvador and Nicaragua may also not be related to the education system at all but could be the result of changes in the labor market and the relative demand for skilled and unskilled labor. The increase in the real earnings of highly educated workers in Costa Rica is likely related to the ability of Costa Rica to export high-technology goods and services. Bashir, Gindling, and Oviedo (2012) show that in Costa Rica, recent export growth has been concentrated in high-productivity skill- and knowledge-intensive goods and services, while in El Salvador and Nicaragua, the bulk of recent export growth has been in unskilled labor-intensive products. Luque and Moreno (2011) divide the evolution of jobs in Costa Rica and Nicaragua between 2001 and 2009 into five categories of occupations: three higher-skill, new economy occupations (nonroutine cognitive analytical, nonroutine cognitive interpersonal, and routine cognitive) and two lower-skill, old economy occupations (routine manual and nonroutine physical). They find that in Nicaragua there has been almost no growth in higher-skill, new economy occupations. Costa Rica, in contrast, achieved impressive growth in higher-skill, new economy occupations that use nonroutine

cognitive analytical and routine cognitive analytical skills. The high level of quality education available to Costa Rican workers, which is related to much higher per student public expenditures on education in Costa Rica compared to the rest of Central America, was a necessary precondition underlying Costa Rica's ability to be successful in developing a thriving high-technology sector.

4. This result might be partly explained by a "selection effect" of the entry cohort; that is, as more students enter upper secondary education, it is likely that the average quality of the students drops, thus leading to a reduction in the level of learning.

5. This is in an environment where total public spending on education in Honduras is high by international standards. The education sector in Honduras accounts for the largest share of public sector spending and for roughly 37 percent of social spending, having reached US$1.4 billion in 2013. Public spending on education represented 5.8 percent of GDP in 2013, but averaged 6.7 percent of GDP between 2007 and 2012, after reaching a historic high of 7.6 percent of GDP in 2009. This expenditure on education is high compared not only to its neighbors in Central America, but also to OECD countries.

6. However, over the last two years, the SEDUC has been implementing and enforcing provisions to halt teacher strikes and ensure compliance with the school calendar. These efforts resulted in achieving, on average, 200 days in 2012 by extending the calendar year about 25 days to compensate for lost days, and reached 213 days in 2013, exceeding the mandatory number of school days by 13. School year 2014 was also on track to surpass the 200-school-day mark.

7. The Organismo Directivo de la Escuela Inclusiva (ODEI) is the most important governing body.

8. Argentina, Brazil, Chile, Colombia, Ecuador, Mexico, and Peru.

9. Efficiency is defined as public sector performance divided by public sector expenditure (see box 5.6).

References

Adelman, M. A., and M. Szekely. 2016. "School Dropout in Central America: An Overview of Trends, Causes, Consequences, and Promising Interventions." Policy Research Working Paper 7561, World Bank Group, Washington, DC.

Afonso, A., A. Romero, and E. Monsalve. 2013. "Public Sector Efficiency: Evidence for Latin America." IADB Discussion Paper 279, Inter-American Development Bank, Washington, DC.

Afonso, A., L. Schuknecht, and V. Tanzi. 2005. "Public Sector Efficiency: An International Comparison." European Central Bank Working Paper 242, European Central Bank, Frankfurt.

———. 2010. "Public Sector Efficiency: Evidence for New EU Member States and Emerging Markets." *Applied Economics* 42 (17): 2147–64.

Bashir, S., T. H. Gindling, and A. M. Oviedo. 2012. *Better Jobs in Central America: The Role of Human Capital.* Washington, DC: World Bank.

Bassi, M., M. Busso, and J. S. Munoz. 2015. "Enrollment, Graduation, and Dropout Rates in Latin America: Is the Glass Half Empty or Half Full?" *Economia* 16 (1): 113–56.

Beneke de Sanfeliu, M., and P. Acosta. 2014. "Programa de Apoyo Temporal al Ingreso (PATI): Evaluación de Impacto." World Bank, Washington, DC.

Bruns, B., and J. Luque. 2014. *Great Teachers: How to Raise Student Learning in Latin America and the Caribbean.* Washington, DC: World Bank.

de Ree, J., K. Muralidharan, M. Pradhan, and H. Rogers. 2015. "Double for Nothing? Experimental Evidence on the Impact of an Unconditional Teacher Salary Increase on Student Performance in Indonesia." NBER Working Paper 21806, National Bureau of Economic Research, Cambridge, MA.

ECD/Inter-American Development Bank/World Bank. 2014. *Pensions at a Glance: Latin America and the Caribbean.* Paris: OECD Publishing.

ERCA (Programa Estado de la Región). 2016. "Quinto Informe Estado de la Region: El dilema estrategico de la educación en Centroamérica." Statistical Appendix. http://www.estadonacion.or.cr/erca2016/.

Fiszbein, A., and N. Schady. 2009. *Conditional Cash Transfers: Reducing Present and Future Poverty.* Washington DC: World Bank.

Gindling, T., and J. Trejos. 2014. "The Distribution of Income in Central America." In *Handbook of Central American Governance*, chapter 3, 75–94, edited by Diego Sanchez-Ancochea and Salvador Marti i Puig. Oxford: Routledge Press.

Luque, J., and M. Moreno. 2011. *Assessing the Evolution of the Skill Structure in Labor Markets in LAC.* Washington, DC: World Bank.

Maluccio, J., and R. Flores. 2005. "Impact evaluation of the pilot phase of the Nicaraguan Red de Protección Social." Research Report 141. International Food Policy Research Institute, Washington, DC.

Mata, C., and K. Hernández. 2015. "Conditional Cash Transfer Impact Evaluation: An Evaluation of the Costa Rican Secondary Education Program Avancemos." *Economics Sciences Journal* 33 (1): 9–35.

Mullis, I. V. S., M. O. Martin, and P. Foy. 2008. *TIMSS 2007 International Mathematics Report: Findings from IEA's Trends in International Mathematics and Science Study at the Fourth and Eighth Grades.* Chestnut Hill, MA: TIMSS & PIRLS International Study Center, Boston College.

UNESCO. 2015. Full Third Regional Comparative and Explanatory Study (TERCE) report. http://www.unesco.org/new/en/santiago/education/education-assessment-llece/third-regional-comparative-and-explanatory-study-terce/.

World Bank. 2015. *World Development Indicators 2015.* Washington, DC: World Bank.

CHAPTER 6

Selected Institutional and Governance Arrangements in the Social Sectors

As shown in chapter 5, while in some countries low social spending presents a problem for substantially improving the quality of the delivery of public social services, in general the few resources spent are not cost-effective. This suggests that there is substantial room to improve efficiency in public spending throughout Central America. In this chapter, we look at the efficiency and effectiveness of the public institutions in charge of social services.

Institutions governing public social programs should be designed in such a way as to ensure continuity of social spending focused on promoting equality of access to high-quality services in a cost-effective manner. In this section, we first discuss some recent institutional reforms in Central America that promote these goals. Then we identify the most important institutional challenges to reaching those goals. In general, the following overarching challenges exist across countries and sectors.

First, institutions that provide public social services are fragmented, with overlapping mandates and lack of coordination, even in countries with legislation and social protection ministries. Second, there is limited flexibility in social spending. It is often not possible to shift resources from programs that are not efficient or effective into programs that are. Third, there is weak accountability, with limited monitoring of the efficiency and effectiveness of social spending and insufficient enforcement of rules and regulations.

In the remainder of this chapter, we discuss, for each sector, examples of recent institutional progress and challenges to the efficient operation of institutions and governance in Central America. These issues were identified and prioritized as being relevant based on the diagnostic and assessments conducted in the individual social sector expenditure and institutional review (SSEIR) country notes.

Education

Progress

In the recent years, some countries in the subregion have strengthened the collection of national student assessments in a more regular and systematic manner. Honduras, Guatemala, and Panama, for example, have joined the Programme for International Student Assessment (PISA). Honduras now also has systematic and regular national student assessments, although results from standardized tests in Honduras show there is still a long way to go to reach satisfactory levels of student achievement. Performance at grades 7–9 are particularly low, with only 34 percent to 40 percent of students reaching satisfactory levels in reading, and just 3 percent to 7 percent of the students reaching a similar level in mathematics. Achieving satisfactory quality levels is a challenge in both rural and urban areas. Interestingly, according to Honduras's national standardized test scores, there are no evident gaps in educational outcomes between students in rural and urban areas. However, since enrollment rates in rural areas are much lower than in urban areas, the rural sample is likely biased toward those with higher motivation and effort to remain in school. In any case, student achievement clearly remains an overall challenge.

To improve school monitoring, El Salvador, Guatemala, Honduras, and Nicaragua also have, on a very small scale, implemented school-level "report cards." School report cards provide information on simple indicators of school characteristics, coverage, quality of teaching, and learning outcomes. One goal of school report cards is to engage parents and other community stakeholders in the process of holding schools accountable. The Civic Engagement for Education Reform in Central America (CERCA) began to publish reports in 2004. Elected parent, teacher, and student representatives, along with principals and community leaders, were involved in collecting data and producing the school report card. School report cards were implemented in 36 schools in the Dominican Republic, El Salvador, Guatemala, Honduras, and Nicaragua.

Although no formal evaluation was conducted, "anecdotal reports from the case studies state that, compared to nonparticipating schools with similar profiles, participating schools experienced higher involvement of community members in school activities...and parents became more engaged in promoting reading and writing, even when they were illiterate themselves" (Bruns, Filmer, and Patrinos 2015).

Finally, on early child development, there is evidence that Nicaragua has been a champion in improving cross-sectoral Human Development coordination across different ministries and in expanding access to preschool across different delivery modes (formal and informal).

Challenges

At the Central American regional level in education, there is little coordination among education authorities, especially on common accreditation and certification. Without a common accreditation and certification process throughout

Central America, education certification in one country may not be recognized in another. Fragmentation of institutions in the education sector is evident within countries. For example, in Panama, the regulatory framework overseeing the education sector is complex and uncoordinated. While the Ministry of Education (SEDUC) centralizes many functions in the system, other actors (the workforce, unions, the private sector, and the public) are gaining powerful influence in the institutional framework and decision-making process. For example, teachers' unions play an important role in the education system and exert political influence through the media, political campaigning, protests, and strikes.

There are limited diagnostics of the effectiveness and quality of teachers and directors, and no systematic monitoring of their performance. For example, all across the region, there is a reduced focus on determining quality standards for new teachers, and there is no evaluation of teachers based on student performance. Nor is teacher pay linked to performance. In general, salaries also tend to be much more tightly distributed than other professions, suggesting that there are few salary incentives for outstanding performance; most teachers receive similar pay whether their performance is good or bad (see figure 6.1 for the example of Panama, in panel a, and Costa Rica, in panel b).

In El Salvador, for example, per-student education spending increased and teachers earn more per hour than other professionals do, but with no monetary incentives to boost learning outcomes, there has been little improvement in test scores. In Honduras, per-student spending is high compared to Latin America, but almost 90 percent of education spending goes to wages. Teacher salaries are high compared to other professionals in Honduras, especially after a 63 percent wage increase in 2009, and teacher salaries did not fall when other public sector salaries fell with overall public spending during 2009–12. In part, this occurred because of politically strong teachers' unions and frequent teacher strikes, which

Figure 6.1 Teachers' Salaries (Hourly Earnings) in Panama and Costa Rica

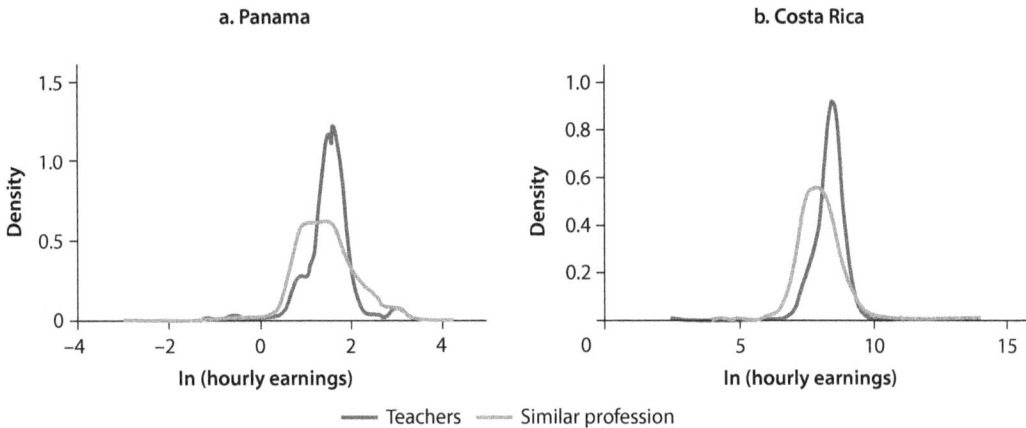

Sources: ENCOVI 2011. Methods used based on Bruns and Luque (2014) and World Bank analysis of household surveys.

Toward More Efficient and Effective Public Social Spending in Central America
http://dx.doi.org/10.1596/978-1-4648-1060-2

decrease the number of effective school days. In Honduras, one-third of the school year of public school students is lost to teacher strikes. Nevertheless, high and growing spending on education and teacher salaries did not translate into improved student education outcomes. The unusually high wage bill also reduced the ability to fund other education resources such as supplies and infrastructure.

Finally, the delivery of in-service training for basic education teachers has improved in some of the countries, but delivery is generally still fragmented across different institutions, and rarely is there a modular curriculum, based on a good diagnostic of the main teachers skills gaps. An illustrative example is Nicaragua (World Bank 2016). More than 80 percent of teachers participate in training programs annually. Ministry of Education (MINED) directorates covering preschool, primary, and secondary schooling frequently prepare in-service training modules and workshops, which are implemented in coordination with the General Directorate of Teacher Training and its territorial delegations. In addition, teachers participate in monthly cluster peer group sessions held to review classroom experience, prepare plans for the following month, and receive training in specific topics chosen by MINED. However, evidence on the cost-effectiveness of these courses is almost nonexistent.

Moving forward, one of the most important areas for reform is to align these trainings with the school curriculums and to adjust the models to the gaps identified in each teacher. Currently, most of the teacher training programs are short and the curriculum theoretical, and there is no focus on classroom management skills. Selected examples of concrete areas for improvement (as discussed in Bruns, Filmer, and Patrinos 2015) include improving mastery of content, improving classroom management, developing strategies for keeping students engaged, and fostering peer collaboration (across and within schools).

Even though the government has recognized some of these challenges, it is still unclear whether and how they will be addressed. The possibility of developing an effective teacher policy is threatened by the lack of an integrated institutional mechanism for coordinating student recruitment for teacher training and other human resource policies within MINED's Instituto Nacional Tecnológico (National Institute of Technology), and the National University Council (Consejo Nacional Universitario, CNU). Working groups of university professors and students from some of the education faculties of the institutional members of the National University Council are currently developing and implementing strategies to strengthen teacher training in both traditional and vocational schools.

Health

Progress

In the health sector, a number of countries have implemented results-based management to improve the quality of public spending on health. For example, Guatemala, Honduras, and Panama have implemented initiatives to improve results-based financing (RBF), with different degrees of success. In Honduras, the Ministry of Health (MOH) has been supporting implementation of decentralized models at the primary level of care, which are managed by community-based organizations, nonprofit NGOs such as foundations, and groups of municipalities known as *mancomunidades* that sign performance-based agreements with the MOH. These decentralized models have the following characteristics: (a) they operate in areas that fulfill a set of socioeconomic criteria, including the poverty level, access to health and education services, and health indicators; (b) they provide a basic package of health services oriented toward prevention and health promotion and basic curative care, prioritizing young children and reproductive-age women; and (c) they are paid based on a formal management agreement between their management entity and the MOH.

The MOH monitors and evaluates the management entity and its facilities using a set of quality and, mainly, production indicators. By 2013, there were 269 health facilities[1] operating under this arrangement in 13 of the country's 18 regional health departments. The number of these facilities has more than doubled since 2008, constituting approximately 15 percent of public ambulatory health facilities in the country. Evidence shows they are generally more productive and provide higher-quality services than MOH facilities. Similar results-based management programs have also been implemented in Panama for primary care, initially under the Paquete Integral de Servicios de Salud (Integrated Package of Health Care Services) in remote, rural, and indigenous areas, using results-adjusted capitation payments to provide financial incentives for providers to achieve better results, and then through the Health Protection for Vulnerable Populations (PSPV) Program, which started in 2008.

Using the same RBF mechanism, the PSPV provides health services to the rural poor through mobile health teams that receive financial incentives to expand coverage and improve performance. Guatemala also implemented a results-based management budgeting process for maternal and child health and nutrition that was recognized for improving the results orientation of public sector health spending. However, its implementation has been affected by delays in funding and capacity constraints in the MOH at the central and departmental levels, in monitoring and providing implementation support to the program.

The use of various alternative modalities of providing health care has contributed to universal coverage in Costa Rica and improvements in health service coverage in underserved areas in other Central American countries. These include the use of mobile health care teams in Costa Rica, El Salvador, Guatemala, Honduras, and Panama; decentralized models for rural PHC in Honduras; and contracting out some health care delivery in rural areas to NGOs in Guatemala and Panama. For example, El Salvador's Network of Integrated Health Care Services supports the strengthening of coverage of health services through implementation of Equipo Comunitario de Salud (Family Community Team; ECOS), which is an organization of health teams that visit rural areas to provide general and specialized health care to households. This service is considered innovative because it harmonized the way PHC was delivered, especially in poor rural areas. Previously, these health services were provided by NGOs, which were costlier and less harmonized, especially with the rest of the health system.

Costa Rica is an example of an integrated health care system with clearly defined functions between the MOH and the Caja Costarricense de Seguridad Social (Costa Rican Social Security Institute; CCSS). The CCSS owns a wide network of hospitals, clinics, and PHC services and purchases all medicines, laboratory reagents, equipment, and other inputs needed to provide individual health care services. The MOH is responsible for health sector stewardship and key public health services, while the CCSS provides individual health care services. At the same time, the CCSS is responsible for selected public health interventions, such as vaccinations and data collection on public health risks at the community level. The private sector provides small-scale ambulatory and diagnostic services to all income groups and inpatient care, mostly to the well off.

There are also ongoing initiatives to improve coordination between the MOH and social security administrations in El Salvador, Guatemala, Honduras, and Panama. These initiatives have had varying degrees of success. For example, in Guatemala and Honduras, there have been efforts to coordinate procurement of medicines between the MOH and the Social Security Institute. In El Salvador, the Social Security Institute and the MOH have an agreement that establishes the mechanisms by which they could work together to address the needs of the insured and uninsured population, but more work needs to be done to implement it. In Panama, progress has been made in coordinating the management of some facilities such as regional hospitals and the new primary care centers in innovative health, as well as human resources. There are also a number of standing collaboration agreements between the Caja de Seguro Social (Social Security Council; CSS) and the MOH in the areas of hospital care, hemodialysis, transplants, oncology, and surgical care, among others.

However, efforts to focus on the level of services to be provided by the CSS and MOH remain unsuccessful. In particular, a law that would have assigned provision of health services at the secondary and tertiary level of care, including hospital management to the CSS, and implementation of PHC programs to the MOH, was not approved. As a result, both entities continue to duplicate services and resources in some areas.

Challenges

Institutional fragmentation is evident in the provision of health care in a number of countries, resulting in the provision of different packages of health services that depend on a person's institutional affiliation. In particular, in El Salvador, the National Health System is highly fragmented and segmented, with parallel health systems based on capacity to pay and involvement in the formal labor market. The MOH, through the Network of Integrated Health Care Services, covers 75 percent of the population, the Social Security Institute 21 percent, and teachers' welfare (Instituto Salvadoreno de Formación, Salvadoran Institute for Professional Training) and Comando de Sanidad Militar (Military Health Unit;

COSAM) about 2 percent each of the population. These institutions do not form a national integrated health service network and do not share responsibilities for the population's health. Per capita expenditures across these entities vary significantly, as do the earnings of their respective target populations. These disparities are reflected in the types and quality of services available to the population (benefits package) and the inefficiencies in the public system. As a result, benefits packages in El Salvador can be very different depending on which of these many organizations a person is affiliated with.

In a number of Central American countries such as Panama, efforts to integrate the two public institutions, the MOH and the CSS, that provide the majority of health services in the country have had limited success, leading to duplication of efforts. The level of coordination between the MOH and CSS in Panama has improved in terms of the management of some facilities (regional hospitals and the new primary care centers in innovative health) and human resources in health. However, both entities continue to run primary, secondary, and tertiary care health facilities across the country, each having its own health information system with independent modules that are not linked across institutions, resulting in a duplication of effort in some areas. Although the CSS is supposed to cover at least 81 percent of the population, the MOH has been reported to also provide health care services to CSS affiliates. Limited coordination between the CSS and MOH has also resulted in the country not being able to take full advantage of economies of scale in the purchase of medicines. This situation is also evident in other countries such as Guatemala and Honduras where the MOH and Social Security Institute have jointly procured medicines on only a few occasions.

There is limited flexibility in social spending partly because budgets are often based on historic levels rather than efficiency and performance. While there have been efforts in the health sector to improve the results orientation of the budget preparation and allocation process, implementation of RBF mechanisms has been focused mainly on PHC (such as in Honduras and Panama) or for specific programs such as maternal and child health and nutrition in Guatemala. None of the countries have actually expanded RBF implementation throughout the sector. However, Honduras plans to progressively expand performance-based financing from decentralized models of care provided by NGOs, community-based organizations, and groups of municipalities to public providers, including hospitals.

Weak accountability is evident in the health sector, for example, in reports of inappropriate use of funds and questionable contract awards in Honduras and Guatemala. Throughout the years, procurement of medicines in Honduras has been subject to frequent allegations of corruption. The government has tried various procurement modalities for medicines including the use of the United Nations Development Programme as a procurement agency, and the establishment in 2006 of the Centro Interinstitucional de Medicamentos (Inter-Institutional Committee on Drugs) to promote transparency in drug procurement. These efforts have not been consistently implemented, however.

Toward More Efficient and Effective Public Social Spending in Central America
http://dx.doi.org/10.1596/978-1-4648-1060-2

The analysis undertaken by the civil society organization Transformemos Salud estimates that, since 2010, the government has lost approximately 300 million lempiras each year through corrupt practices in the procurement of medicines (Transformemos Salud 2014). Furthermore, the serious drug shortage in 2013 led the government to make emergency purchases of medicines to meet the pressing needs in major health centers and hospitals. This, in turn, led to a government investigation of the MOH's central warehouse. The investigation revealed serious internal control issues, including falsification of supply requests and records and of stocks of expired medicines that were not distributed on time to health facilities.

In Guatemala, there have been reports of ghost employees (for example, in 2015, MOH investigations found 18 ghost posts within the ministry itself; a majority of the posts were for legal advisers); contract awards that did not meet technical standards (for example, 17 of 21 refurbishment or rehabilitation contracts did not meet minimum requirements established by law); and leakages in the form of medical supplies stolen from some facilities. The incarceration of the former Instituto Guatemalteco de Seguridad Social (Guatemalan Institute of Social Security; IGSS) board in 2015 for awarding a contract to a firm that provided equipment and medicines that did not meet technical requirements and that caused medical complications in a number of patients is a positive step in enforcing accountability in the sector.

Social Protection and Labor

Progress

In the area of social protection, most countries have invested substantial resources in building unique registries of beneficiaries of social programs, which can allow them to rationalize and improve program effectiveness. These registries are more developed in some countries than in others. For instance, Costa Rica has a relatively developed system, including a national beneficiary registry and the use of poverty maps. The Sistema de Atención a Beneficiarios (Beneficiary Attention System; SABE) in Costa Rica is an integrated system that includes the entire process the beneficiary goes through, from initial attention to the delivery of benefit. The Registro Único de Beneficiarios (Unique Beneficiary Registry; RUB) is the national registry of beneficiaries that aims to maintain a current database and national coverage data with information of all people requiring services, assistance, grants, or financial aid, finding themselves in situations of poverty or need. Honduras is developing a registry of beneficiaries of social programs that will help avoid duplication of beneficiaries and better target social interventions.

In 2010, the Secretaría de Desarrollo Social (Secretary of Social Development; SDS) started developing a national beneficiary registry (Registro Único de Beneficiarios) under its new information technology platform (Centro Nacional de Información del Sector Social, National Center for Information on the Social Sector; CENISS). The RUB database composed of beneficiaries of most social programs (including Bono 10,000 beneficiaries) is expanding, reaching 1.9 million by the end of 2012, but still its use has been limited due to limited enforcement and visibility of the instrument, and financial constraints to complement the database with a census of nonbeneficiary house-holds through a single registry instrument (Ficha Socioeconómica Única).

Coordination in the social sector has been advanced in a number of countries by the creation of a Ministry of Social Development or interinstitutional coordi-nating councils. For example, the lead institution in the social protection and labor (SPL) sector in Panama is the Ministry of Social Development (MIDES). Its institutional appearance has been the result of the reorganization of what was the Ministry of Youth, Women, Children, and Family. MIDES manages most of the major SPL interventions in Panama such as the conditional cash transfers (CCTs) and the Social Pension.

A Ministry of Social Development was created in Guatemala in 2012, which is now the leading institution in the SPL sector and has inherited the administra-tion of the main social assistance interventions. The ministry has been established as the governing body of the social sector, responsible for designing and establish-ing national policies oriented to enhance the well-being of socially vulnerable groups including the unemployed youth and children with unmet nutritional requirements, among others. It is also accountable for developing national strate-gies to optimize food security, education, and health services throughout the country, and it is expected to coordinate with the different sectors and subna-tional levels of government to deliver such services.

Costa Rica has developed an interinstitutional council to facilitate interagency coordination. The council is chaired by the vice president and consists of the Presidency of the Republic, the newly created Ministry of Human Development and Social Inclusion, the Ministry of Labor and Social Security, the SEDUC, the MOH, the Ministry of Culture and Youth, the Ministry of Housing, the National Institute for Women, and the Costa Rican Institute of Sport and Recreation. The council will be implemented by the Instituto Mixta de Ayuda Social (Mixed Institute of Social Aid, IMAS).

In Honduras, the SPL sector previously comprised several uncoordinated execut-ing institutions reporting to various levels and an SDS, created in 2006 to provide oversight but with a weak mandate and few resources. A major reform in 2014 changed the landscape of the sector. A Social Inclusion and Development Cabinet chaired by the Secretary of Social Inclusion and Development (former SDS) was created with a much stronger mandate than in the past to lead the implementation of the *Vida Mejor* strategy, an umbrella framework for social policy, providing a social protection floor and prioritizing the 835,000 families in extreme poverty.

Most of the countries have been investing heavily in improving their SPL monitoring and evaluation mechanisms. Honduras has done this by creating and consolidating the RUB, through the identification and geographical mapping of social protection interventions (Registro de Oferta Institucional; ROI), and by establishing the Sistema Único de Evaluación de Políticas Públicas Sociales (Unified System for the Evaluation of Social Public Policies; SUEPPS) to track and follow key management and performance indicators of interventions.

El Salvador has made efforts similar to those of Honduras, and importantly has complemented them with a system to track and follow key management and performance indicators of interventions. Moreover, it has made the evaluation of the impact of key interventions a top priority for management, starting with the CCT, PATI, social pension, and school uniform programs.

These efforts have not been implemented at the same pace across all Central American countries. In Nicaragua and Guatemala, for example, little is known about the impact of interventions and the basis for an efficient budget allocation.

Challenges

Despite attempts to consolidate programs and institutions, institutional fragmentation is still the norm in SPL. This is manifested in both the social insurance and pension sector and in the social assistance sector. In pensions, several schemes coexist with no strong justification and miss important synergies to avoid creating the wrong incentives. An example is Guatemala, which has a disability, old age, and survival plan; a special scheme for public workers; and another for the military, plus a social pension scheme. Similar arrangements exist in Costa Rica and Honduras.

Costa Rica, in particular, is a case in institutional fragmentation in the SPL sector and also an example of failed attempts to address the issue. The current institutional and budgeting setting is complex, consisting of several uncoordinated institutions without clear leadership or accountability. For instance, two separate agencies are implementing nutrition and food security programs. Services and benefits provided even within the same institution are not necessarily comprehensive and complementary; instead, they are dispersed, duplicated, and fragmented. It has distinct budgetary processes in the public sector.

First, there is the central government budget or national budget, which is approved by the Legislative Assembly. Second, there is the budgetary process of the institutions outside the central government whose budgets are approved by the Comptroller General of the Republic and which doubles the size of the national budget. Budgets are also increasingly constrained by constitutional mandates and rules, such as directives on minimum spending for education, municipalities, housing subsidies, and community development. Additional laws stipulate that portions of taxes and fees must be allocated to certain activities and institutions. More important, the executive has no power to direct or contain spending in autonomous institutions since they operate with wide margins of budgetary and administrative independence and are constitutionally protected from political interference or changes in government.

Employment services are weak and virtually absent from the role of labor intermediation for the majority of vulnerable groups. Despite attempts to strengthen employment services, only recently have the Ministries of Labor in the Central American region begun to move away from exclusive roles of monitoring compliance with labor standards and regulations toward facilitation of labor intermediation. The latter efforts are nascent and promising, but still weak and usually under resourced, understaffed, and not well connected with the needs of the private sector.

Among the best examples are Honduras, with its *Empleate* services in regional employment offices. Each regional and employment office collects information on job openings and posts job opportunities online for job seekers to apply for, matching the labor demand needs of the private sector with a registry of unemployed people. So far, these employment offices have captured labor demand needs of formal firms but not of informal small and medium enterprises, due to legal restrictions. As a consequence, the current labor intermediation system has primarily served the population with secondary or university education and is still limited in coverage. Therefore, less educated individuals still face serious information constraints when looking for a job, and they do not generally access counseling and job search assistance programs.

Another limitation is the lack of "employment of last resort" mechanisms, such as social investment funds or workfare (low wage public employment), to activate in times of emergency. On that front, only El Salvador, through the PATI, has been able to provide such opportunities with meaningful coverage, also in coordination with employment offices in targeted municipalities. Only the Ministry of Labor and Social Security of Costa Rica has managed to implement several labor market programs for entrepreneurs and to offer financial and training assistance for its beneficiaries. Aside from provision of training, other employment services of ALMPs with meaningful coverage are still negligible in Guatemala, Nicaragua, and Panama.

Note

1. These are primary-level care facilities consisting of 172 rural health centers, 68 urban health centers, 28 maternal and child clinics, and 1 adolescent clinic.

References

Bruns, B., F. Filmer, and H. A. Patrinos. 2015. *Making Schools Work: New Evidence on Accountability Reforms*. Washington, DC: World Bank.

Bruns, B., and J. Luque. 2014. *Great Teachers: How to Raise Student Learning in Latin America and the Caribbean*. Washington, DC: World Bank.

Transformemos Salud. 2014. "Corrupcion en Compra de Medicamentos Provoca Pérdidas Anuales de 300 Millones: Transformemos Honduras." *Proceso Digital*. http://proceso .hn/index.php/component/k2/item/87337-corrupci%C3%B3n-en-compra-de -medicamentos-provoca-p%C3%A9rdidas-anuales-de-300-millones-transformemos -honduras.

World Bank. 2016. "Nicaragua Social Sector Expenditure and Institutional Review (SSEIR) Note, P158442—Nicaragua and Guatemala Notes—Central America Social Sector Expendi." World Bank, Washington, DC.

CHAPTER 7

Policy Recommendations

This chapter presents selected policy recommendations derived from our expenditure and institutional analysis in Central America. It starts by presenting recommendations for education, health, and social protection and labor, including country-level discussions when needed. The chapter concludes with recommendations that are applicable across sectors and several countries in the subregion.

Education

Spending in the subregion should increasingly focus on improving the quality of basic education to ensure strong foundations, namely increasing the quality of teachers to foster learning outcomes. All countries in the subregion have achieved near-universal primary coverage rates (gross enrollment rates range from over 100 percent in Costa Rica to almost 70 percent in Guatemala), but there remains a need to rebalance spending toward higher-quality basic education. Policies to improve pedagogies and teacher instructional quality are promising and range from attracting the best professionals into teaching and preparing teachers with useful training and experience, to strong principals and master teachers motivating them to perform (see Bruns and Luque 2014). However, especially in the short run, some of these reforms to strengthen learning assessments and use them to guide other policies, including teachers do not seem immediately politically feasible given the strong teachers' unions.[1] Moving forward, almost all countries can improve the cost-effectiveness of their in-service teacher training programs by developing quality standards or coupling academic training with practical on-the-job learning. In addition, there is substantial room to improve measurement and accountability by improving monitoring of student outcomes and teacher performance.

The investment in strengthening teacher *quality* and accountability will require different solutions across different countries. For example, in Costa Rica, a large supply of university degrees to prepare teachers led to an excess supply of teachers and a huge variation in teacher quality. As a consequence, there are many teachers working outside the profession, and the ones that teach benefit from reasonably high wages. Establishing quality standards, possibly through an entry exam, might raise the quality of teaching at all levels. In other countries, such as Honduras and Nicaragua, enhancing the skills of existing teachers through, for example, more cost-effective in-service teacher training, might be more effective. Honduras, in particular, could benefit from an aggressive skills development strategy for both teaching and nonteaching staff.

In other countries such as El Salvador, a key need is to attract new, qualified teachers to the workforce. In the case of El Salvador, creating special financial incentives to attract top students to the teaching profession and raising accreditation standards for university-based programs of teacher training are appropriate. In Guatemala, supporting the training programs combining classroom and hands-on teachers' practices (as seems to be the case with the Professional In-service Teacher Training Program, PADEP/D) and linking it to career progression of teachers also seems to be a relevant policy.

Strengthen the collection and use of data, including national student assessments, for policy design and evaluation of management and information systems in education. Having a solid education management and information system that assesses and tracks inputs, resources, governance, operations, and outcomes of its education system is therefore critical. Some countries, such as Costa Rica and Honduras, have taken important steps in that direction. However, almost everywhere it is lacking a systematic approach. One example is Panama, where an education census has not been regularly collected and where participation in international student assessments were, until recently, rare and ad hoc. In addition, Guatemala could strengthen the monitoring and evaluation capacity at the local levels, especially the use of the information reported in the learning assessments and school report cards for policy purposes (in a systematic and regular way). Hence, the subregion could increase the effectiveness of public education spending by improving data collection, data and systems management, and most importantly, the use of data in decision making, ultimately improving learning for all children and youth.

Invest more resources in preschool access and quality. Extensive research shows that increased access to high-quality early childhood education improves school readiness and retention in higher grades, increasing the effectiveness of the spending (Carniero and Heckman 2003). Learning deficits begin early, grow over time, and are exacerbated by financial constraints. There is well-established evidence that high-quality early childhood development programs act as equalizers, because they can reduce the effect of household socioeconomic differences on the child's cognitive and noncognitive development and, thus improve his or her ability to perform well in school. This is especially true for disadvantaged children. Especially in rural areas, there is also a need for high-quality parenting programs to support the early cognitive and socioemotional development of children to get them school ready. One example is the reforms underway in

Nicaragua, where there has been an expansion of early childhood education services; the number of education centers receiving children ages 3–5 is growing rapidly. Much of the expansion has come from a recognition of, and subsequent support for, informal preschools created at the community level by local organizers, donor-supported NGOs, and volunteers. The formalization of grassroots institutional development has been more rapid than the creation of new formal teaching posts. The government has opted for a semiformal alternative based on the payment of a monthly "volunteer stipend" of approximately US$30 to finance preschool teachers, plus a subsequent complement through a República Bolivariana de Venezuela-financed "solidarity bonus" of about US$40. The key question is whether the government will commit the resources necessary to incorporate available teachers into the formal system.

Support an improvement in graduation rates and increase the completion rates in secondary education by developing better diagnostic tools to screen student barriers and developing more compressed support packages (including selected demand- and supply-side interventions) for the most complex and hard-to-reach groups. Spending on secondary education is rising in most Central American countries, but not by enough. Relative to GDP per capita, public spending on secondary education is low relative to the Latin American average, while spending on primary and tertiary education is high. The evidence in the chapter shows that in the subregion, one of the major challenges is to first do a better and earlier assessment of the reasons for dropping out of secondary school and, for the most vulnerable groups, develop more comprehensive and diverse strategies accounting for the actual differences in the reasons for dropping out across countries. For example, in Costa Rica and Panama, the focus should be on improving upper secondary completion rates, while in other Central American countries, it is necessary to improve both lower and upper secondary completion rates. Within countries, the reasons for dropouts differ between boys and girls and by region and income, and so should policies.

For countries that face more barriers for completing lower secondary education, such as El Salvador, Guatemala, Honduras, and Nicaragua, Almeida, Fitzsimons, and Rogers (forthcoming) suggest that the most successful demand-side interventions will be those related to information campaigns and conditional cash transfers (CCTs). Hence, in those countries, a promising demand-side approach would be to expand and redesign the existing CCTs to condition payments on enrolling and keeping students in lower secondary school. The evidence shows that CCTs in Honduras and Guatemala (in Central America) and in Argentina, Colombia, Mexico, and other Latin American countries, which condition on primary school attendance, have proven effective in increasing primary school enrollment and graduation. A CCT in Costa Rica focused on improving lower and upper secondary enrollment and graduation (including increased monetary transfers for upper secondary schools compared to lower secondary schools) has been effective in increasing enrollment and attendance in upper secondary schools. El Salvador, Guatemala, Honduras, and Nicaragua could also benefit from the promotion and dissemination of information on the economic returns of completing secondary education to students. This could be done specially for at-risk groups, whom are more likely to have less information. Returns to education are generally higher than for most other investments. The goal is to convince myopic students of the value of staying in school in the long term. A study in Mexico notes that many teenage students **have little or no family pressure or guidance and they see that one in every two of their peers drop out of high school in part because they do not have information about the potential returns of education.** When they make education decisions, it is through a distorted perspective where they severely underestimate the labor market returns to education. As a result, there is an underinvestment in education in the form of less effort, less schooling, or both (Avitabile and de Hoyos 2015).

For El Salvador, Guatemala, Honduras, and Nicaragua, there are also promising supply-side interventions such as community school-based management (SBM) and full-time schools. Community SBM transfers the management of schools from central authorities to the principals, teachers, parents, students, and other school community members. Randomized controlled trial evaluations of SBM programs have found that they improve educational outcomes. Currently, most public schools offer their students a day of four to five hours, allowing for double shifts. Typically, full-time school programs extend, by three to four hours, the time students spend in school in the afternoon, also offering lunch. Several evaluations of full-day school programs find positive impacts on graduation and dropout rates.

In countries like Costa Rica and Panama, the issues seem to be more on the completion of upper secondary education. Here, Almeida, Fitzsimons, and Rogers (forthcoming) suggest that the most promising interventions on the demand side are "deferred" scholarship and teen pregnancy reduction programs (for females). One set of programs would be to keep young mothers in school through day care in school, CCTs, and extended school hours. Other programs should be directed to keep teenage girls from becoming pregnant. One effective intervention is to provide girls with information on the returns to schooling so that they do not think their only option is to become mothers (see discussion in Almeida, Fitzsimons, and Rogers [forthcoming]). In addition, deferred scholarships that offer a substantial portion of the reward only after students have met major benchmarks, combined with early partial payment, may also provide an incentive to students with little conception of future costs and benefits. This could be particularly effective for improving upper secondary completion rates.[2] Costa Rica has an effective CCT directed toward reducing upper secondary dropout rates, *Avancemos*. Yet, *Avancemos* reaches only 29 percent of 15–19-year-olds from the poorest income quintile. A better targeting of subsidies and transfers can significantly weaken the liquidity constraints that affect poor households.

For Costa Rica and Panama, promising supply-side interventions relate to improving socioemotional learning and strengthening tutoring in schools. Socioemotional (cognitive behavioral) training with supplemental academic tutoring to improve school retention and completion have been shown to be effective. "Cognitive-behavioral interventions (CBIs) refers to interventions used to change behavior by teaching individuals to understand and modify thoughts and behaviors. Problem solving, anger control, self-instruction, and self-control are examples of interventions under the umbrella of CBI. A central aim of CBIs is to improve social skills and problem-solving abilities, enabling young people to cope better with challenges and reducing the likelihood that they will develop depressive symptoms when faced with stress. In these programs, for example, students may learn to recognize difficult situations that have produced inappropriate or violent responses in the past, and to identify and implement acceptable responses. Students also learn to restrain aggressive behavior using covert speech. By practicing these skills through various teaching and role-playing activities, students will learn to more consistently engage in appropriate behavior when faced with situations that have caused problems in the past" (Almeida, Fitzsimons, and Rogers [forthcoming]).

Reduce the violence that surrounds secondary school and the peer influence of criminal gangs on secondary school students. The influence of youth gangs has a negative impact on the ability of young men and women to remain in secondary school, especially in El Salvador, Guatemala, and Honduras.

While within-country inequalities in access are present across all countries, they are especially acute in Guatemala and Panama. In Guatemala, enrollment rates are much lower for rural and indigenous students, and within rural areas, especially for girls. While most countries have achieved near-equal outcomes for boys and girls, in Guatemala, girls make up only 45 percent of primary and secondary students. Panama is also a country where, although average education levels are high, indigenous populations have limited access to education. For countries with high dropout rates at the lower secondary level, such as Guatemala, Honduras, and Nicaragua, one supply-side focus should also be on improving the quality of primary education. If students do not come to secondary school prepared, they are likely to drop out.

Reduce inequalities in access to higher education and foster regional integration and coordination and regional dialog in education certification and accreditation mechanisms, especially for higher education and technological education. Spending on, and access to, tertiary education throughout the subregion is biased toward students from high-income families. It is important to expand access to tertiary education to lower-income students. In addition, stronger regional coordination in accreditation of tertiary education is necessary to ensure higher returns to tertiary education, even if students migrate to other countries. Because Central American countries are small, there are large gains in economies of scale to be realized in regional coordination for the quality certification and accreditation of technical and higher education skills (including technological education). Regional integration and cooperation in tertiary education can be a major catalyst for far-reaching progress. The European Bologna Process, which is designed to ensure comparability in the standards and quality of European higher education qualifications, illustrates the great potential and spillover effects of cooperation in tertiary education, from raising quality standards

Toward More Efficient and Effective Public Social Spending in Central America
http://dx.doi.org/10.1596/978-1-4648-1060-2

and fostering academic partnerships and research collaboration to strengthening international mobility, understanding, and human capital. There is a latent potential for a similar process in LAC and for Central America.

Health

Continue to expand service coverage while also prioritizing improvements in the quality of health care. Most Central American countries have successfully increased access to health care, although coverage gaps still exist in rural areas and for poor, indigenous segments of the population in a number of countries. While access still needs to be expanded, the main challenge is to improve the quality of care. Providing free services in public facilities will not have the intended impact of eliminating or significantly reducing out-of-pocket costs if patients still need to seek care in private facilities because public facilities are not sufficiently staffed and stocked with medicines they need for treatment. For most Central American countries, this would mean having sufficient numbers of skilled health staff provide services based on established health protocols in all areas, and health facilities that are adequately equipped and stocked with medicines and supplies. In Costa Rica, the main challenge would be how to provide timely care and minimize the waiting times for specialized services.

Central American countries need to continue to expand and strengthen primary health care (PHC) services in rural areas. All Central American countries except for Costa Rica—which has already achieved universal PHC access—would need to expand their PHC services, and all Central American countries need to improve the quality of these services. Most Central American countries still need to enhance prevention and health promotion efforts to improve maternal and child health and nutrition and prevent infectious diseases while also confronting the increasing threat of noncommunicable diseases (NCDs). Costa Rica needs to pay particular attention to improving its NCD prevention and control efforts. A number of countries also need to review the sustainability of interventions such as decentralized PHC services in Honduras and Family Community Teams (ECOS) in El Salvador.

Prepare and implement strategies to reduce disparities in health packages and per capita spending across institutions and progressively move toward integrating the national health system. For example, Costa Rica achieved universal coverage through the expansion of a single social insurance scheme, the CCSS (*Caja Costarricense del Seguro Social*), which currently covers about 90 percent of the population. This level of coverage was achieved partly through to the successful integration of social insurance (for the formal sector) and the Ministry of Health (MOH) (for the nonformal sector), whereby the former absorbed the facilities of the latter during the 1990s. The MOH is responsible for health sector stewardship and key public health services, while the CCSS provides individual health care services. Still, there is also room to improve management at the central level of the CCSS, which has six division managers who tend to work in silos. Creation of a CCSS general manager position would improve CCSS management.

Improve management information systems and their use at all levels.
Timely and reliable information plays an essential role in planning and management of services. All countries in Central America are using health information systems, but the challenge is the lack of integration or at least having interoperability among the information systems used by different health institutions. A number of countries, such as Guatemala, also face challenges in terms of underreporting of information, especially from facilities in rural, more isolated areas, and information flows, which tend to flow up to the central level with limited feedback provided to lower administrative levels. Countries could develop and implement an action plan to strengthen operational links among information systems and modules, and progressively enhance integration and use of information for evidence-based planning, decision making, and supervision support at all administrative levels.

Progressively improve efficiency and results orientation of planning, budgeting, and management of resources. Countries could enhance the impact of the public funds they invest in health by implementing various mechanisms to improve efficiency based on their country context. For example, in Honduras, build on positive experiences and lessons learned in PHC decentralized models and progressively expand performance agreements between the MOH and other public providers. In Panama, review the different results-based budgeting approaches used under different schemes to develop one coordinated results-based budgeting mechanism for rural and poor areas. In El Salvador, assess the existing budgeting and planning process to determine how best to move away from the traditional historically based resource allocation approach toward a more results-oriented one. In Costa Rica, in the short term, gradually introduce prospective payment mechanisms that allow for increased transparency in hospital services. Capitated payments to networks could be introduced over time to improve equity and efficiency.

Implement human resources management strategies to better address inequities and improve results. To attract more and better-qualified health staff, the health and education sectors would need to work together to improve the relevance of the curriculum and teaching quality, to attract more students and trainees from rural and indigenous areas, and to reduce dropout rates. For the health sector to retain health workers, countries could provide performance incentives and enforce accountability measures while also improving supportive supervision.

Given the fiscal constraints in most Central American countries, the availability and distribution of health sector staff could be improved by (a) assessing the feasibility of offering more nonmonetary incentives (such as housing provided by local authorities/communities or special training) to complement some monetary incentives to attract staff to work in rural and remote areas; and (b) applying M-Health[3] and the use of cellular phones at primary and secondary service delivery levels as a way to address human resources and physical access constraints.

To improve accountability and, in turn, health worker performance, countries could consider (a) establishing a consolidated human resources database for permanent and contractual staff to be tracked by department, municipality, and facility (it is recommended that this list be periodically verified by a random staffing audit to reduce the incidence of ghost employees); (b) implementing measures to prevent and control the hiring of staff without a confirmed budget to pay their salaries on time; and (c) implementing a standardized and transparent process of evaluating staff performance with well-defined incentives and sanctions that are systematically applied.

Strengthen pharmaceutical procurement and management and develop an integrated policy on medicines. Given that medicines represent a significant share of out-of-pocket costs in most countries in Central America, there is a need to improve the overall institutional capacity of the sector to manage pharmaceuticals and ensure the availability of essential drugs, especially in primary care centers. In the short term, technical specifications of bidding documents need to be improved. In a number of countries, the availability and adoption of standardized, common bidding documents and a common essential drugs list for all public entities, especially the MOH and the Social Security Institute, could contribute to increasing economies of scale and procurement of medicines at lower prices. Over time, countries could move toward implementing an integrated public policy on medicines together with actions to improve planning, budgeting, procurement, distribution, and monitoring to enhance the availability and affordability of medicines.

Continue to mobilize additional public financing for health in countries where there are significant coverage and quality gaps. While public funds could be reallocated based on efficiency gains from improvements in human resource management and drug procurement such as those mentioned above, additional funds would still be needed to improve coverage and quality, as well as overall implementation capacity, especially in Guatemala and Honduras. In particular, although Guatemala is already using taxes on tobacco and alcohol sales to finance health services, the overall level of public funds allocated to the health sector remains low, which limits the country's ability to invest in infrastructure and staff to reduce its significant delivery gap. Honduras is considering taxing soft drinks, although it is not clear whether this would produce sufficient revenue to cover the financing gap needed to improve coverage and quality of services. These countries could research the experience of other countries that have taxed other sectors, such as mobile phone companies, and used the funds for health.

Develop a strategy to effectively integrate NCD prevention into PHC. Given that NCDs have emerged as among the leading causes of deaths, and their corresponding negative impact on disability-adjusted life years and health care costs, it would be important for countries in Central America to adopt a more proactive approach and strengthen preventive and health promotion services. The context of each country must be considered. In El Salvador, for example, the government could develop a strategy to effectively incorporate NCDs into its PHC program, while in Guatemala, the challenge would be how to effectively implement its new PHC model, which now includes NCD prevention and control.

In Nicaragua, the MOH needs to take the lead in the preparation of public policies to address risk factors for chronic diseases. In Panama, the government could determine a set of actions to properly identify the elderly population at risk for NCDs and crosscheck beneficiary data to determine whether they are enrolled in existing social protection programs. In Costa Rica, the government could improve prevention and effective management of NCDs at the primary level of care, and also identify and strategically address the main drivers of dramatically escalating costs in NCD treatment and care.

Social Protection and Labor

Central American social security systems, which account for the bulk of social protection and labor (SPL) spending, are clearly not delivering what they promised; coverage is still low (due to high labor informality) and their fiscal sustainability is in serious question. As happens in many other Latin American countries, but which is exacerbated in Central America due to a higher incidence of labor informality, coverage of contributory pension systems is particularly low and regressive (mostly benefiting the upper-income quintiles because they are the only ones capable of contributing to the system).

At the same time, the fiscal costs of contributory pensions for resource-constrained governments in the Central American region is enormous. In some cases, this is due to generous subsidies, particularly for public sector employees who can retire with replacement rates that are higher than average for LAC, and even for OECD countries (Costa Rica, Guatemala). In others, failed reforms did not deliver what they promised, and even generated onerous transition costs that current generations are still paying (El Salvador). Almost all pension systems in the Central American region have serious funding deficits and contingent liabilities that require urgent reforms to avoid a major drag on fiscal accounts that would crowd out other needed spending in basic delivery of social sector services or subsidies to the poor. This problem, unless tackled urgently, can become unmanageable with the aging of the population and the increase in the dependency ratio (dependents over active population).

Most countries in the subregion have expanded access to social assistance, mostly through cash transfers and social pensions narrowly targeted toward the poor, but there is still ample room for better resource allocation to these programs from untargeted subsidies. All countries now have noncontributory (social) pension programs that provide basic pension payments to low-income elderly who did not contribute to the pension system while they worked. In addition, throughout this report we have discussed CCT programs, which exist in all countries and have adequate targeting performance. Nonetheless, coverage of both among the poor is still low in most Central American countries, and in some cases is erratic (as in Guatemala and Honduras, with beneficiaries frequently coming in and out of the program due to implementation challenges).

In comparison, consumption subsidies are expensive and have significant benefits to nontarget groups. Reforming consumption subsidies can free up resources for better-targeted and more efficient programs. It is also critical to continue both monitoring and evaluation of programs, and investing in information systems to better target beneficiaries, such as social beneficiary registries.

While rigorous evaluations of the effectiveness of several CCTs have been undertaken, regular evaluations are not yet the norm in the majority of SPL interventions. The widespread use of rigorous evaluations and local training in evaluation has the potential to significantly improve efficiency by identifying programs that work and those that do not. In the case of CCTs, it has been useful to push for a reform agenda to improve effectiveness and highlighting areas of improvement (including how impact increases when implementation performance improves, conditionalities are properly monitored, and payments are delivered regularly). Unfortunately, aside from CCTs, the majority of other SPL interventions did not follow through with this trend, and little is known about their impact on improving the welfare of the poor.

There are also important links between the success of CCTs and reforms in other sectors. For example, for CCTs to improve education and health outcomes, quality education and health care must be available. The success of social sector improvements also depends on spending on other public infrastructure programs; a focus only on social spending may not be effective if it is not accompanied by spending in other sectors. For example, transportation infrastructure (that is, roads) is necessary for the public to be able to access health facilities, schools, and training programs. A functioning communications infrastructure (that is, telephones) and information technology infrastructure (that is, internet networks) can facilitate all types of social spending.

Active labor market policies should also be revamped and made more relevant for the unemployed population and labor market entrants. Coverage of ALMPs is low, and more efforts are needed to reach the most vulnerable populations. The current institutional setting for the occupational training system provides little information on the quality and adequacy of existing training programs, limiting the efforts of better matching existing skills and those needed in the market. Typically, low-skilled workers are not properly served by these interventions, which focus only on formal jobs for the highly skilled.

It is also critical to complement services to include self-employment promotion and mentoring activities. With regard to training, targeted programs are required for young people who currently have low educational levels or who will be likely to drop out of school, to complement education sector policies. However, many public training programs have focused mainly on employed and unemployed adults. Countries of the region could benefit from a toolkit of workfare programs, with respective operational guidelines, to be quickly implemented in times of economic crisis and natural disaster, especially in urban areas. The model of El Salvador's Temporary Income Support Program (PATI) could be explored for increasing opportunities for emergency temporary employment during times of crisis while at the same time promoting access to training opportunities for the low-skilled and poor, often excluded from mainstream interventions.

Similarly, many countries are exploring piloting or expanding "productive inclusion" or "graduation" programs for a more sustained exit from poverty, but as the evidence shows, this is a complex area that, to succeed, requires multipronged and well-coordinated approaches among different institutions. (El Salvador and Costa Rica are currently more focused on trying to set up large coverage schemes for youth employment and income generation promotion).

Cross-Sectoral and Cross-Regional Messages

The subregion needs to strengthen monitoring and evaluation systems across the social sectors. This can be achieved by building stronger monitoring and evaluation mechanisms that track the registration of students and beneficiaries as early as possible, and that track the take-up of the different services. This tool is important to evaluate which programs are effective and efficient so that spending can be directed to those programs, and to improve or eliminate programs that are not effective.

Strengthen accountability of the public service provision to focus on "human development" results. This includes systematic enforcement of incentives and accountability measures and ensuring periodic reporting of results to citizens. It also includes encouraging active citizen involvement to promote transparency and accountability (for example, social audits, community scorecards, and innovative feedback mechanisms through cell phones). Means of monitoring and evaluating programs can be built into program design. It is important to know which programs are effective and efficient to direct spending to those programs and eliminate programs that are not effective.

Reallocate resources to better serve those in geographic areas with less access. Location is important. Access to education, health, and social protection services is lower in rural and indigenous areas in all countries. Efforts should be strengthened to improve access in these areas.

Strengthen coordination within the social sectors to increase the availability of qualified human resources. For example, to increase the availability of qualified health sector staff, the education and health sectors would need to coordinate better to enhance the practical relevance of the quality of curriculums and teaching; attract more students and trainees, especially from rural, indigenous communities; and reduce dropouts.

Notes

1. Examples of reforms that almost all countries could benefit from include improving the processes of recruitment, retention, and teacher evaluation to ensure countries have more motivated and qualified teachers. Addressing the strong compression of teachers' wages by linking teacher evaluations and performances with results, ultimately increasing the attractiveness of the profession for many who value career and wage progression, could also be an important step.

Toward More Efficient and Effective Public Social Spending in Central America
http://dx.doi.org/10.1596/978-1-4648-1060-2

2. Evaluation of the *Oportunidades* program in Mexico suggests that for a scholarship program for secondary students with myopia about the future or a lack of interest in studies to be effective, short-term incentives to remain in school are important. Dropout rates in upper secondary schools might also be reduced through a redirection of the focus of CCTs.

3. M-Health is the practice of medicine and public health with mobile devices.

References

Almeida, R., E. Fitzsimons, and H. Rogers. Forthcoming. "How to Prevent Secondary-School Dropout in Latin America: Evidence from Rigorous Evaluations." Unpublished mimeo.

Avitabile, C., and R. de Hoyos. 2015. "The Heterogeneous Effect of Information on Student Performance: Evidence from a Randomized Control Trial in Mexico." World Bank Policy Research Working Paper 7422, World Bank, Washington, DC.

Bruns, B., and J. Luque. 2014. *Great Teachers: How to Raise Student Learning in Latin America and the Caribbean*. Washington, DC: World Bank.

Carniero, P., and J. J. Heckman. 2003. "Human Capital Policy." IZA Discussion Paper 821, IZA, Bonn.

Survey Sources, by Country

Country	Period	Surveys	Education	Social protection	Labor	Health
Costa Rica	2007–14	Encuesta de Hogares de Propósitos Múltiples (Multiple Purpose Household Survey; EHPM) 2007–09; Encuesta Nacional de Hogares (National Household Survey; ENAHO) 2010–13; Encuesta Nacional de Salud (National Health Survey; ENSA) 2006; Encuesta de Ingresos y Gastos (National Income and Expenditure Household Survey) 2012–13	EHPM, ENAHO	EHPM, ENAHO	EHPM, ENAHO	Encuesta Nacional de Ingresos y Gastos de los Hogares (National Income and Expenditure Household Survey; ENSA)
El Salvador	2007–13	Encuesta de Hogares de Propósitos Múltiples (Multiple Purpose Household Survey; EHPM) 2007–12	EHPM	EHPM	EHPM	EHPM
Guatemala	2006, 2011, 2014	Encuesta Nacional de Condiciones de Vida (ENCOVI) 2006, 2011, and 2014	ENCOVI	ENCOVI	ENCOVI	ENCOVI
Honduras	2007–13	Encuesta Permanente de Hogares de Propósitos Múltiples (EPHPM) 2007–13; Demographic Health Survey (DHS) 2011–12	EHPM	EHPM	EHPM	DHS
Nicaragua	2005, 2009, 2014	Encuesta de Medición de Niveles de Vida (Welfare Measurement Survey; EMNV)	EMNV	EMNV	EMNV	EMNV
Panama	2007–13	Encuesta de Hogares (ECH) 2007–09; Encuesta de Mercado Laboral (Labor Market Survey; EML) 2010–12; Encuesta Nacional de Niveles de Vida (ENV) 2008	ECH, EML	ECH, EML	ECH, EML	ENV

Environmental Benefits Statement

The World Bank Group is committed to reducing its environmental footprint. In support of this commitment, we leverage electronic publishing options and print-on-demand technology, which is located in regional hubs worldwide. Together, these initiatives enable print runs to be lowered and shipping distances decreased, resulting in reduced paper consumption, chemical use, greenhouse gas emissions, and waste.

We follow the recommended standards for paper use set by the Green Press Initiative. The majority of our books are printed on Forest Stewardship Council (FSC)–certified paper, with nearly all containing 50–100 percent recycled content. The recycled fiber in our book paper is either unbleached or bleached using totally chlorine-free (TCF), processed chlorine–free (PCF), or enhanced elemental chlorine–free (EECF) processes.

More information about the Bank's environmental philosophy can be found at http://www.worldbank.org/corporateresponsibility.

green
press
INITIATIVE

www.ingramcontent.com/pod-product-compliance
Lightning Source LLC
Chambersburg PA
CBHW080425270326
41929CB00018B/3165